INTRODUCING
ISSUES WITH
OPPOSING®
VIEWPOINTS

Depression

David M. Haugen, Susan Musser,
and Michael Chaney, *Book Editors*

GREENHAVEN PRESS
A part of Gale, Cengage Learning

GALE
CENGAGE Learning·

Farmington Hills, Mich • San Francisco • New York • Waterville, Maine
Meriden, Conn • Mason, Ohio • Chicago

Elizabeth Des Chenes, *Director, Content Strategy*
Cynthia Sanner, *Publisher*
Douglas Dentino, *Manager, New Product*

© 2014 Greenhaven Press, a part of Gale, Cengage Learning

WCN: 01-100-101

Articles in Greenhaven Press anthologies are often edited for length to meet page requirements. In addition, original titles of these works are changed to clearly present the main thesis and to explicitly indicate the author's opinion. Every effort is made to ensure that Greenhaven Press accurately reflects the original intent of the authors. Every effort has been made to trace the owners of copyrighted material.

Cover image © Peerayot/Shutterstock.com

LIBRARY OF CONGRESS CATALOGING-IN-PUBLICATION DATA

Depression / David M. Haugen, Susan Musser, and Michael Chaney, book editors.
    pages cm. -- (Introducing issues with opposing viewpoints)
    Summary: "Introducing Issues with Opposing Viewpoints: Depression: Introducing Issues with Opposing Viewpoints is a series that examines current issues from different viewpoints, set up in a pro/con format"-- Provided by publisher.
    Includes bibliographical references and index.
    ISBN 978-0-7377-6921-0 (hardback)
    1. Depression, Mental. 2. Depression in adolescence. 3. Depression in children. I. Haugen, David M., 1969- editor of compilation. II. Musser, Susan, editor of compilation. III. Chaney, Michael P., 1957- editor of compilation.
    RC537.D4263 2014
    616.85'27--dc23
                                                                            2013048064

Printed in the United States of America
1 2 3 4 5 6 7 18 17 16 15 14

Contents

Chapter 3: What Treatments Should Be Used to Address Depression?

Foreword

I ndulging in a wide spectrum of ideas, beliefs, and perspectives is a critical cornerstone of democracy. After all, it is often debates over differences of opinion, such as whether to legalize abortion, how to treat prisoners, or when to enact the death penalty, that shape our society and drive it forward. Such diversity of thought is frequently regarded as the hallmark of a healthy and civilized culture. As the Reverend Clifford Schutjer of the First Congregational Church in Mansfield, Ohio, declared in a 2001 sermon, "Surrounding oneself with only like-minded people, restricting what we listen to or read only to what we find agreeable is irresponsible. Refusing to entertain doubts once we make up our minds is a subtle but deadly form of arrogance." With this advice in mind, Introducing Issues with Opposing Viewpoints books aim to open readers' minds to the critically divergent views that comprise our world's most important debates.

Introducing Issues with Opposing Viewpoints simplifies for students the enormous and often overwhelming mass of material now available via print and electronic media. Collected in every volume is an array of opinions that captures the essence of a particular controversy or topic. Introducing Issues with Opposing Viewpoints books embody the spirit of nineteenth-century journalist Charles A. Dana's axiom: "Fight for your opinions, but do not believe that they contain the whole truth, or the only truth." Absorbing such contrasting opinions teaches students to analyze the strength of an argument and compare it to its opposition. From this process readers can inform and strengthen their own opinions, or be exposed to new information that will change their minds. Introducing Issues with Opposing Viewpoints is a mosaic of different voices. The authors are statesmen, pundits, academics, journalists, corporations, and ordinary people who have felt compelled to share their experiences and ideas in a public forum. Their words have been collected from newspapers, journals, books, speeches, interviews, and the Internet, the fastest growing body of opinionated material in the world.

Introducing Issues with Opposing Viewpoints shares many of the well-known features of its critically acclaimed parent series, Opposing Viewpoints. The articles are presented in a pro/con format, allowing readers to absorb divergent perspectives side by side. Active reading questions preface each viewpoint, requiring the student to approach the material thoughtfully and carefully. Useful charts, graphs, and cartoons supplement each article. A thorough introduction provides readers with crucial background on an issue. An annotated bibliography points the reader toward articles, books, and websites that contain additional information on the topic. An appendix of organizations to contact contains a wide variety of charities, nonprofit organizations, political groups, and private enterprises that each hold a position on the issue at hand. Finally, a comprehensive index allows readers to locate content quickly and efficiently.

Introducing Issues with Opposing Viewpoints is also significantly different from Opposing Viewpoints. As the series title implies, its presentation will help introduce students to the concept of opposing viewpoints and learn to use this material to aid in critical writing and debate. The series' four-color, accessible format makes the books attractive and inviting to readers of all levels. In addition, each viewpoint has been carefully edited to maximize a reader's understanding of the content. Short but thorough viewpoints capture the essence of an argument. A substantial, thought-provoking essay question placed at the end of each viewpoint asks the student to further investigate the issues raised in the viewpoint, compare and contrast two authors' arguments, or consider how one might go about forming an opinion on the topic at hand. Each viewpoint contains sidebars that include at-a-glance information and handy statistics. A Facts About section located in the back of the book further supplies students with relevant facts and figures.

Following in the tradition of the Opposing Viewpoints series, Greenhaven Press continues to provide readers with invaluable exposure to the controversial issues that shape our world. As John Stuart Mill once wrote: "The only way in which a human being can make some approach to knowing the whole of a subject is by hearing what can be said about it by persons of every variety of opinion and studying all modes in which it can be looked at by every character of mind. No wise man ever acquired his wisdom in any mode but this." It is to this principle that Introducing Issues with Opposing Viewpoints books are dedicated.

Introduction

Depression is an illness the brutality of which is matched only by its perverseness. Estimates vary, but it is likely that close to one in six people can expect to struggle with it at some point in their lives. The symptoms are cruel—including insomnia, hopelessness, loss of interest in life, chronic exhaustion, and even an increased risk of physical ailments such as heart disease. Depression also leads people to cut themselves off from others, a tendency exacerbated further by the continuing stigma surrounding the condition, thought to deter over half of depressed people from seeking treatment. Untreated, depression can lead to suicide; the World Health Organization (WHO) estimates there is one suicide every forty seconds. These factors all contribute to the WHO's assessment of depression as the leading cause of disability in the world.

In its mildest state, depression indicates a listless or downhearted mood that might follow a sad event, such as the death of a friend or relative, or stem from an unfulfilling pursuit, such as lackluster employment or unrequited love. While such feelings can alter a person's outlook and daily habits, they tend to pass fairly quickly after a time of mourning, reflection, and readjustment; however, if these gloomy emotions persist, they may suggest the presence of one of the more potent and debilitating forms of clinical depression. Clinical depression is a medically recognized disorder in which a sufferer exhibits melancholy, anxiety, or even self-destructive behaviors for prolonged periods. The roots of clinical depression are not definitely known and vary from person to person; however, researchers believe depression stems from a combination of biological and genetic factors as well as environmental stress.

Similar to mild depression, the symptoms of clinical depression can include feelings of sadness and lowered self-esteem, but individuals hampered with this illness might also display fatigue and decreased energy, loss of interest in hobbies or activities, irritability and lack of concentration, gain or loss in appetite, insomnia or excessive sleep, feelings of worthlessness, or thoughts of suicide. Psychologists have learned how to treat depressive disorders through therapy and medications, and those who receive professional assistance often overcome the incapacitating effects of the illness and return to more normal routines. Unfortunately, though, many who live with clinical depression go undiagnosed because they believe their symptoms are "normal" or are embarrassed about seeking help. Seeking help can be difficult for people who suffer clinical depression, but experts agree that most types of this disorder can be successfully regulated if they are diagnosed and treated.

Because individuals and their experiences are unique, clinical depression can manifest in different ways. For Jamie Flexman, a music teacher and blogger for the *Huffington Post*, depression is a feeling of mental and physical sluggishness—"and nothing can snap you out of it." He insists that it is important to distinguish clinical depression from generic sadness or just having a bad day. "It isn't a change in mood related to a trivial life event," Flexman writes in a September 18, 2013, post. He describes it as becoming "trapped inside your own prison and true access to your brain lies behind that locked door. Sometimes, briefly, you are allowed outside to stretch your legs but you know this is temporary. Eventually you will have to return to your cell and wait patiently for a time when you are given another opportunity to function like a normal member of society. There is no choice in the matter." Flexman emphasizes the recurring nature of his own depressive symptoms, and it is common for those who have any of the various forms of depression to fear that the negative feelings might return even if the illness is treated.

The National Institute of Mental Health (NIMH) categorizes depressive illnesses by severity, duration, and circumstance. Minor depression, for example, denotes the persistence of less-severe symptoms for a period of two weeks or longer, though such symptoms can recur once the period ends. Major depression, on the other hand, signifies a bout of depressive symptoms that significantly impair daily functioning, including one's ability to sleep, eat, and work, for example. Major depression can be a onetime, destabilizing event, or it might return in cycles over a lifetime. According to the NIMH, 6.7 percent of adults and 3.3 percent of teenagers in the United States have experienced severe depression at some point in life. Between minor depression and its catastrophic counterpart rests dysthymia, a form of depression which is usually less disabling than a bout of major depression but can last for years. The NIMH notes that those who live with minor depression or dysthymic depression can experience episodes of major depression as well.

In addition to these more commonplace classifications, the NIMH includes other disorders that contain some of the traits and symptoms of depression. Seasonal affective disorder (SAD) typically afflicts sufferers during the dark, winter months. It can be treated with light therapy, and it tends to pass naturally when daylight increases in the springtime. Postpartum depression affects some new mothers because of hormonal and physical changes in the body and because of the sudden onset of responsibility that comes with caring for an infant. Psychotic depression applies to individuals who are depressed and suffer some detachment from reality such as irrational beliefs or the hearing of voices. Finally, manic-depressive illness (now offically called bipolar disorder) is often diagnosed in those sufferers who have cyclical, sweeping mood changes from manic highs to depressive lows. Like their conventional cousins, all of these atypical depressive illnesses can be effectively treated with drugs and therapies if the would-be patients are willing and able to engage medical assistance.

Treating depressive disorders often requires a combination of mental health counseling and prescription drugs. Psychotherapists help depressed patients understand their illness and provide strategies to overcome the negative feelings and dour outlook associated with it. In the most severe cases, however, counseling may not be enough. Doctors may prescribe drug therapies—particularly antidepressants— to those who suffer major depression or psychotic episodes.

Antidepressants impact chemicals in the brain that regulate mood. Exactly why antidepressants work is still something of a mystery. Researchers commonly believe that reuptake inhibitors, for example, retard the absorption of neurotransmitters by brain cells. The theory holds that the longer the neurotransmitters remain active as communicators between brain cells, the better the brain can maintain tranquil moods. Tetracyclics—another class of drugs—keep neurotransmitters from binding to cell walls so that the levels present between cells rise and effect a similar positive outcome.

Because these theories are unproven, there is some debate in the scientific community over the true benefits of drugs that alleviate depression. Some psychologists contend that the prescribing of antidepressants might create a placebo effect in patients, inducing them to believe the drugs help simply because they are prescribed by a doctor. In a July 14, 2011, article for *Psychology Today,* psychiatrist Steven Reidbord claims that the placebo effect may be compelling even though he nonetheless attests to the transformation of patients who take these drugs. "Thousands—millions?—of individuals claim relief from [using] antidepressant treatment, and virtually any psychiatrist will swear that antidepressants really have helped many of his or her depressed patients," he writes. "Meanwhile, there are also many patients, equally depressed, who obtain little or no benefit from antidepressants, and a large number of carefully conducted studies that find little benefit in the active ingredients of these pills, once placebo effects are factored out." Regardless of whether the active ingredients work, Reidbord affirms, "if a patient feels better, I don't worry too much about who or what gets the credit."

Antidepressants are one option in the fight against depression. Other therapies avoid drugs entirely and focus on persistent, mindful strategies to change habits and attitudes to move forward on a day-to-day basis. Indeed, most doctors and patients agree that depression is an ongoing battle even when treatment helps sufferers regain their lives. Other suggested remedies to help stave off the effects of depression include dietary changes, regular exercise, spending time outdoors, engaging in meaningful activities, listening to music, and staying connected with other people. The merits of all these are subject to debate, but there is an overriding expectation that finding ways to stay positive will only benefit those who want to counter the negative impulses that depression engenders. In *Introducing Issues with Opposing Viewpoints: Depression,* various experts and interested commentators debate some of the contested issues surrounding depression and its treatment. In giving voice to these debates, this anthology reveals how much of the neuroscience is uncharted and how many of the treatments remain unproven. For the 14.8 million American adults who live with clinical depression, the outcomes of these debates have significance beyond any rhetorical victories. While the lack of consensus might underscore the fact that science still has no firm answers regarding some key aspects of the illness, it also indicates that the struggle to understand this disorder continues in hope of finding them.

Chapter 1

Is Depression a Serious Problem?

Individuals living with depression face many of the same problems as those with life-threatening physical diseases such as cancer.

Depression Is a Real Illness

Robert Packard

"*Depression ... exists as surely as does cancer and, for its victims, is no less real.*"

Robert Packard argues in the following viewpoint that while depression is often viewed as an illness that is less serious than other, physical diseases, individuals living with depression face many of the same problems as those with life-threatening diseases such as cancer. He asserts that depression can grow and spread throughout one's life in the same way as cancer does, that depression can be treated with specific approaches just like cancer, and that depression can have the same life-threatening consequences as cancer. Packard urges individuals suffering from the symptoms of depression to take the disease seriously and seek medical help to ensure that they do not lose their lives to this illness. Robert Packard is a student at Piedmont Virginia Community College in Charlottesville, Virginia, and assistant editor at the college's student-run newspaper, the *Forum*.

AS YOU READ, CONSIDER THE FOLLOWING QUESTIONS:

1. According to the author, how many Americans experience clinical depression?
2. In Packard's opinion, what is the difference between depression and cancer?
3. What does the author believe to be the danger in viewing depression as less "real" than physical diseases?

I am depressed. Not literally at this moment, while I write these words, but in general. I am one of approximately 15 million Americans who suffer from clinical depression and yet, by some sardonic [mocking] twist of irony, my diagnosis, by its very nature, makes me feel all alone.

But, I am not alone. At least, I am consciously aware that I am not. See, the nature of depression is that it tricks one's mind into a bleak prison where one's own thoughts play both inmate and warden: interest becomes something to be feigned, not felt; motivation becomes a taunting reminder of one's perceived shortcomings; even hope and self-worth become more foreign concepts than physics to a poetry major.

Depression Grows and Spreads Like Cancer

Like cancer, depression metastasizes, silently seeping into every aspect of one's life. What starts as a melancholy disposition grows—festers—until it is overwhelming. Forget holding down a job, or even doing chores around the house; for the sufferer of depression, just crawling out of bed to take a shower seems a Herculean task akin to climbing Mount Everest.

The author says that, like cancer, depression "metastasizes," silently seeping into every aspect of one's life.

Also like cancer, the threat of recurrence remains ever present. One is never "cured" of the illness fully; he or she only learns to manage it. Just as a cancer survivor should regularly visit a doctor for blood work to determine if their cancer is returning, those suffering from depression must be vigilant in their care, lest they fall back into the hole they have tried to escape.

Unfortunately, however, there is a very significant area in which those fighting cancer and depression differ: their public perception. The physiological effects of cancer are usually readily noticeable, and those fighting them are given a due sense of respect and care. Cancer is, after all, a physically identifiable invader.

Depression sufferers are not so, for lack of a better word, lucky; theirs is an illness that hides. It is an invisible invader. There is no "depression tumor" that can be surgically removed and examined; no treatable parasite dictating the woebegone whims of the mind. But, depression does not exist solely as a figment of the imagination. It exists as surely as does cancer and, for its victims, is no less real.

Depression Must Be Taken Seriously

Although its causes are not yet fully understood, we can point to the symptoms of depression. According to the fourth edition of the *Diagnosis and Statistical Manual of Mental Disorders*, these include "feeling guilty, hopeless, and worthless; having recurring suicidal thoughts; having trouble sleeping, either too much or too little; experiencing appetite [or] weight changes; having trouble paying attention and concentrating; feeling little energy or unexplained tiredness; [and] agitation or slowing down of body movements." Experiencing a combination of these for five weeks or more would meet the requirements to be diagnosed depressed.

At this point, I should mention that the exact causes of cancer are also still under study. Cancer is diagnosed when it presents symptoms—

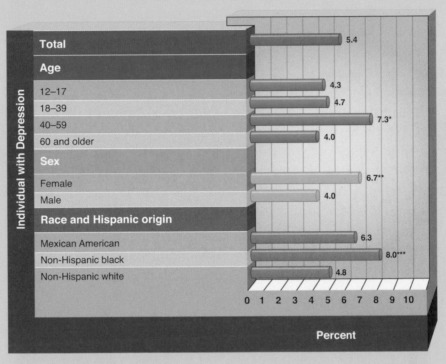

Percentage of Individuals Age Twelve and Older with Depression in the United States, 2005–2006

Individual with Depression

Total	5.4
Age	
12–17	4.3
18–39	4.7
40–59	7.3*
60 and older	4.0
Sex	
Female	6.7**
Male	4.0
Race and Hispanic origin	
Mexican American	6.3
Non-Hispanic black	8.0***
Non-Hispanic white	4.8

0 1 2 3 4 5 6 7 8 9 10

Percent

*Significantly different from all other age groups.
**Significantly different from men.
***Significantly different from non-Hispanic white persons.

Taken from: Centers for Disease Control and Prevention, National Center for Health Statistics. National Health and Nutrition Examination Survey.

benign or malignant—and treatment is taken from there. Friends and families are often more than happy to point these out and advise a medical consultation, as they should, but when it comes to pointing out the signs of depression, the same advice is seldom given.

I cannot, nor will I, claim to speak for everyone here, but my own experience is that depression, and other mental illness, is viewed as somehow less "real" than its physical counterparts. The victim often falls prey to the false belief that, through behavior modification or mere "positive thoughts," the depression will abate. Further, should this fail, the problem lies not with the method of recovery, but with the patient, who has failed to magically moderate his or her maladies with meditation.

This kind of thinking is worse than misguided, it is dangerous and potentially lethal. Medications to lessen the effects of depression are available, as are therapists with whom feelings can be worked out. Treatment does exist and, quite frankly, the prognosis is far better for a victim of depression than one of cancer. But, just as cancer gone undetected can quickly kill, depression left unattended can easily lead to suicide.

I know these things because, as I said at the beginning of this article, I suffer from depression. I share them with you, dear reader, to preface a humble request: If you think you may be depressed, please go see a doctor; if you think your friend may be, urge him or her to make that appointment. Depression is more than just being sad, it is a real, debilitating illness. One as real, and sometimes as deadly, as cancer.

EVALUATING THE AUTHOR'S ARGUMENTS:

Robert Packard begins this viewpoint by stating that he suffers from depression. Do you think that because he has experienced the illness firsthand, he is more qualified or less qualified than someone without depression to make a comparison between depression and cancer? How does this compare with your evaluation of the viewpoint of the following author, Irina Webster, who is a doctor?

Depression Is Not a Real Illness

Irina Webster

In the following viewpoint Irina Webster argues that depression is not a real illness but is actually the body saying that something in one's life must be changed. Webster says that to feel good, people need to listen to their intuition and practice healthy activities such as eating right, getting plenty of rest, exercising, and maintaining good relationships. She insists that listening to one's intuition is the best way for an individual to determine what to do with his or her life, and by listening to it, one can prevent depression and enjoy a healthy and happy life. Webster acknowledges that severe loss and trauma can lead to depression in even the healthiest individuals but contends that a person with depression can recover much faster by following his or her intuition. Webster is a medical doctor and a medical intuitive (someone who uses intuition to diagnose and treat disease) who focuses on women's and children's health. She offers advice on her website, DrIrinaWebster.com.

> *"I don't consider depression as an illness."*

AS YOU READ, CONSIDER THE FOLLOWING QUESTIONS:
1. What seven factors does the author list as being necessary to feel good?
2. What does Webster say is the function of intuition?
3. What are three of the side effects given by the author that can be brought on by antidepressants?

I don't consider depression as an illness. Contrary to its definition I believe that depression is just an adaptive mechanism which has served humans for thousands [of] years.

We all get depressed from time to time. Some people recover faster than others. Some turn to alcohol, drugs, food or something else to cope with their bad feelings. But many are able to find hope and good spirits in a relatively short time: these are normally people who are adept at listening to their intuition or their intuitive voice.

Depression Signals Something Is Wrong

The fact is that feeling low sometimes is nature's way of telling us that something is wrong with our lives and we need to fix it. Depression is similar to pain. Pain tells us that something is wrong with our body and it needs treatment. The same can be said about depression—it warns us that we need to change the way we live our life.

Generally in order to feel good, seven important factors must be present in our lives:

1. Good nutrition.
2. Fresh air.
3. Sunshine.
4. Physical activity.
5. Purposeful activity (goals or purpose in life).
6. Good relationships.
7. Good and regular sleep.

If any of these factors are missing, a person feels uncomfortable. If several of them are missing a person gets depressed and even goes into despair.

The fact is that most depressed people live on a bad diet, drink lots of alcohol, smoke, and stay indoors nearly all the time; they don't exercise and don't have any goals to strive for. Their relationships are poor or almost non-existent.

People Must Listen to Their Intuition

Why do people practice this self-destructive behavioural pattern?

I think one of the most important reasons is that they stop listening to their intuitive voice or their spirit. They lose hope that they can be happy again, have love and feel pleasure. Their intuition shuts down.

Intuition is our gift from nature and its function is to keep us safe, healthy and happy. Our intuitive voice always guides us to what is best for us. This voice is gentle, subtle and non-intrusive. The problem is

Exercising is one of seven factors the author claims are necessary to feel good.

that it can be easily overrun by brain noises—most of which are loud, emotional and negative. The brain is your chatterbox.

The brain tells you how bad your life is, how insufficient you are and how bad you feel. The brain does not necessarily tell the truth but often gives us only a perception of the truth. Intuition always leads you into a better direction in life and always tells the truth.

Of course severe loss and trauma can cause depression even in an otherwise healthy person. Even when all the seven factors are present, the loss of a loved one or a breakup usually result in profound feelings of depression. The same can happen with the loss of one's career, health, home, etc.

But if the person who is suffering the loss is able to connect to his/her intuition—the depression goes away much faster.

One of the worst things that can happen to a person is when they go to a mental health centre, mentions they are depressed and is then sent off to see a psychiatrist. Then they get a prescription for an anti-depressant and are told (falsely) that their depression is an illness like diabetes, for example.

Then they are told they must take pills the same way that a diabetic must take insulin and they lose touch even more with their intuition.

Depressed people take the prescribed drugs they are given, but remain unequipped to manage their lives. Their habits and lifestyle stay the same so the depression grows. The side effects of taking antidepressants can also cause severe problems like drug addictions, drowsiness, immobility, poor coordination etc.

Spiritual Well-Being Leads to Happiness

The most important thing for a mental health professional is to assess a depressed person's lifestyle, habits, relationships, history, etc., to

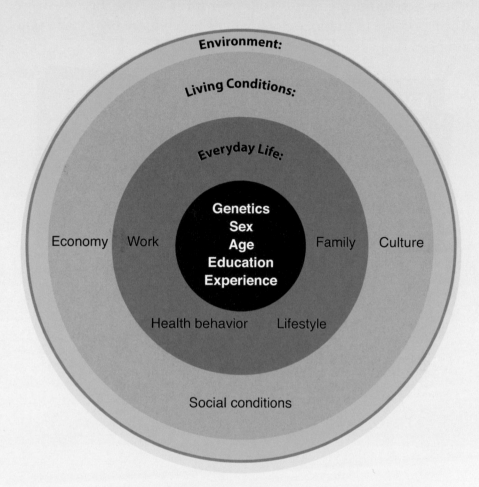

Environmental and Psychological Causes of Depression

Environment:

Living Conditions:

Everyday Life:

Genetics
Sex
Age
Education
Experience

Economy   Work   Family   Culture

Health behavior   Lifestyle

Social conditions

Taken from: UC Davis Health System. "Why Do People Get Depression?" Chronic Disease Care Management and Education.

determine the source of their depressive feelings. From this assessment, a healing program should be developed and active support and assistance provided to the patient in the implementation of this program.

An explanation on how the spiritual side in human beings work must also be provided by a health professional. Without recognising and accepting the spirit it is nearly impossible for anyone to recover from depression permanently. Sure they can go into a kind of remission, but some little thing happens and they crash back to their depression.

The best antidepressant is your own spirit and the intuitive voice we all possess. Learning to use it will be much more beneficial in the long run that a handful of drugs.

EVALUATING THE AUTHOR'S ARGUMENTS:

Do you think Irina Webster's opinion on depression oversimplifies the problem? Why or why not? How does her opinion differ from Robert Packard's viewpoint that depression is as serious as cancer?

Viewpoint

3

Depression Is Bad for One's Physical Health

John Folk-Williams

"Depression . . . greatly increases the risk of developing other serious diseases."

In the following viewpoint John Folk-Williams contends that depression affects not only one's psychological well-being but also one's physical well-being, making it necessary to find a cure for depression. The author describes the most common physical symptoms of depression, of which pain is primary. In addition to the physical problems stemming from depression, Folk-Williams outlines the connection between the diseases that most commonly coexist with depression, including coronary heart disease, loss of bone mineral density, and diabetes, and gives reasons why they are often diagnosed in the same individuals. Folk-Williams has battled depression throughout his life and writes about his experiences in various blogs in the hope of helping others find solutions to their own depression.

AS YOU READ, CONSIDER THE FOLLOWING QUESTIONS:
  1. What does Folk-Williams identify as the physical complaints
     that people with depression most often report to their doctors?
  2. By how much does one's risk of experiencing a "major cardiac
     event" increase after being diagnosed with depression, according
     to the author?
  3. In the study cited by the author, what connections were shown
     to exist between depression and diabetes in the women who
     were studied?

Just as I was thinking I understood the full range of depression's impact on my life, I started finding out about links between the mood disorder and some nasty physical problems. I mentioned in [a previous blog] post the prevalence of pain among depressed people seeking treatment from their regular doctors. But depression can do a lot more to your body than inflict pain. It has been linked to coronary heart disease, congestive heart failure, diabetes and loss of bone mineral density.

The link between the mood disorder and physical impacts, however, isn't a simple matter of cause and effect. Some physical problems, like chronic pain, may be symptomatic of depression, although it's not yet listed among the formal diagnostic criteria for a major depressive episode. When depression appears along with cardiovascular disease, congestive heart failure or diabetes, on the other hand, the relationship is not that of symptom to illness. Instead, depression coexists, or in medical terms, is comorbid, with independent diseases. It can be a risk factor for the future onset of those conditions, and depression may have the same neurochemistry that causes them.

Here are a few of the facts and theories emerging from recent studies.

Pain Is Common with Depression

The most common physical complaints that depressed people bring to their primary care physicians are pain, gastrointestinal problems and sleep disorders. The leader of the pack is pain.

It comes in many varieties that relate to depression. Chronic back pain, joint pain, arm and leg pain, especially when they seem to have no explanation, are high on the list. In fact, the presence of pain and other physical symptoms that seem to have no cause makes it all the more likely that there is an underlying mood disorder, most often depression.

Why does pain, in particular, so frequently appear with depression? Neuroscience researchers have looked closely at the link. Apparently, there's an overlap between pathways in the nervous system that help bring on both pain and depression. The neurotransmitters serotonin and norepinephrine, familiar as the targets of antidepressant medication, also contribute to pain. The evidence seems to say that reduced levels of these hormones can result in both pain and depression.

Unfortunately, treatment usually doesn't deal directly with pain. However, research is finding that if those problems stay with you after you feel better and seem to be out of a bad episode, you have a greater risk of relapsing. That makes me wonder if I've recovered as fully as I thought, since I have my own checklist of chronic physical problems.

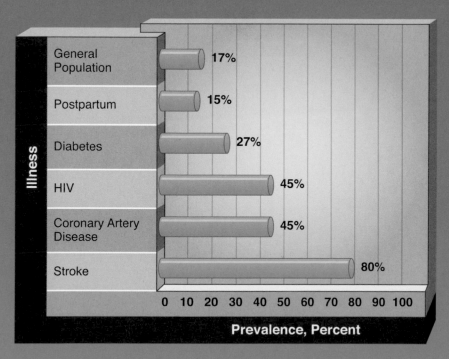

Prevalence of Depression in Individuals with Another Illness

Illness

General Population — 17%
Postpartum — 15%
Diabetes — 27%
HIV — 45%
Coronary Artery Disease — 45%
Stroke — 80%

0 10 20 30 40 50 60 70 80 90 100

Prevalence, Percent

Taken from: Murray H. Rosenthal. "The Challenge of Co-Morbid Disorders in Patients with Depression." *JADA* Supplement 4, vol. 103, no. 8, August 2003.

Depression Often Coexists with Heart Disease

Because heart disease is such a widespread killer, researchers have put together a lot of data about the difference that depression makes to heart patients. The findings aren't good. If you're depressed and have coronary artery disease, you're twice as likely as those who are not depressed to have a major cardiac event within 12 months of the

An angiogram showing the narrowing of the coronary artery in heart disease. According to the author, a depressed person who also suffers from coronary artery disease is twice as likely as someone with coronary artery disease who is not depressed to have a major cardiac event within a year of the depression diagnosis.

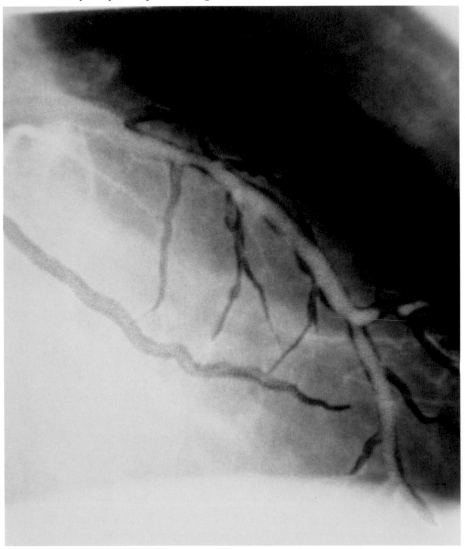

diagnosis. You are also a lot more likely to die after a heart attack or coronary bypass surgery. While a number of studies confirm those grim connections, it's less clear why depression has these effects.

One theory points to impacts on the autonomic nervous system. This is the system regulating vital functions that occur without your awareness, especially the beating of your heart. One part of the autonomic system is the sympathetic nervous system. Its function is to stimulate the heart, while the parasympathetic nervous system relaxes it. Depression may increase the stimulation and reduce the relaxation of the heart muscle, and that can lead to a number of cardiac events.

The neurotransmitters linked to depression could affect the arteries as well. When their levels in the blood drop, that reduction may contribute to the chronic inflammatory process that defines coronary artery disease.

> **FAST FACT**
>
> Of those adolescents in 2011 who experienced a major depressive episode, as defined by the National Survey on Drug Use and Health, 69 percent found that they had significant problems in at least one of the following areas: home, school/work, family relationships, and social life.

Bone Loss Is Common in Depressed People

All studies haven't reached the same conclusions, but the majority of them have found connections between depression and decreases in bone mineral density. That leads to osteoporosis and an increased risk of fracture in older adults.

Depression is linked to elevated levels of the steroid cortisol. Too much cortisol may also affect bone metabolism and so reduce mineral density. Estrogen and testosterone production are important for bone health, and depression tends to lower the levels of these hormones as well. A third mechanism by which depression can lead to bone loss is the increased activity of the sympathetic nervous system that affects heart disease.

The behavior of depressed people can also play a role. Depression is associated with less physical activity, and without exercise the body loses an important way of increasing bone mineral density. Smoking and alcohol use are both linked to depression, and both can reduce bone formation.

Depression and Diabetes Create a Cycle of Illness

About 23 million people in the US have diabetes, and a ten year study, lasting from 1996 to 2006, has found a link with depression. The study tracked more than 65,000 women between 50 and 75 years old. Those who were taking antidepressants were 25% more likely to develop diabetes than women who were not depressed. Women with diabetes were almost 30% more likely to get a depressive disorder than women without diabetes. If they were taking insulin, the risk of depression was more than 50% higher.

There are two ways of explaining this connection. One is biological and has to do with the effects of stress. Depression tends to put people into long-lasting stress, and that results in higher levels of cortisol in the blood. That's the steroid produced by the body to help it deal with threats and high stress situations—which can be psychological as well as external. High levels of cortisol cause numerous problems, and diabetes may be one of them.

The other explanation focuses on the behavior of people with both conditions. Diabetics rely on self-care, including regular insulin injections, and depressed people often fail to take care of themselves. Diabetes can also worsen depression because it is a chronic illness that increases the level of stress and worry in daily life. Since these are also characteristics of depression, they become even worse with the added complication of diabetes.

Early Treatment Can Prevent Other Illnesses

I first read about the possible effects of depression on these widespread diseases in [American psychiatrist] Peter Kramer's *Against Depression*. He argued that such physical effects made it all the more urgent to begin depression treatment as early as possible. Successful treatment of depression at its first appearance increases the chances of preventing the illness from becoming recurrent. And it is the continuing distortion of the body's neurochemistry caused by repeated episodes of depression that greatly increases the risk of developing other serious diseases later in life. That's a strong motive for finding effective treatment as soon as possible.

EVALUATING THE AUTHOR'S ARGUMENTS:

In this viewpoint John Folk-Williams presents extensive statistics and medical data about the relationship between depression and other physical diseases. How does this viewpoint compare with the one written by Robert Packard comparing depression to cancer? Has your opinion about Packard's view changed after reading Folk-Williams's? Why or why not?

Is Depression Actually Good for You?

Rebecca Hardy

"Many people say they emerge [from depression] more resilient and able to take control of their lives."

In the following viewpoint Rebecca Hardy argues that depression can be a force for good in people's lives. Citing many health professionals and referring to a recent study on depression, the author explains how depression has been shown to make many of its sufferers stronger and more resilient. Hardy asserts that many people will get depressed at one time or another in their lives but that by coping with these setbacks they can learn how to survive and even thrive in a sometimes turbulent world. Hardy does admit that many times the reports of feeling better after depression are skewed because they are relative to the severe pain people feel from the illness, but she returns to the research that shows that most people do recover from depression and do not have recurrent episodes. Hardy is a journalist who has written about health and food for a variety of magazines and newspapers, including London's *Independent*.

AS YOU READ, CONSIDER THE FOLLOWING QUESTIONS:
1. According to one Dutch study cited by the author, in what ways did depression help people to cope with life's trials?
2. According to Hardy, what can prevent antidepressants from working?
3. What is the one thing that all experts agree is crucial to one's recovering from depression, as reported by Hardy?

We constantly hear how depression is blighting our lives, but some experts have an interesting, if controversial, theory: depression can be "good for us", or at least a force for good in our lives.

To anyone in the grip of depression, which can vary from mild to severe, this may sound absurd—offensive even. Clinical depression—a very different animal to "unhappiness" or "feeling low"—is a disabling, frightening illness that can ruin people's lives and shake them to their core, but experts say that, for some people at least, there can be benefits.

"If you have depression, which, by definition, is a paralysis of motivation, it will be hard to see any positive outcome," says Marjorie Wallace, founder and chief executive of SANE, who had depression herself. "But I believe that people who go through it come out stronger. It can act as a catalyst to survival because you have looked over the precipice and seen the abyss."

This may sound like wishful thinking, but the argument has been aired before: two years ago Professor Jerome Wakefield from New York University caused a stir when he argued in his book *The Loss of Sadness: How Psychiatry Transformed Normal Sorrow Into Depressive Illness* that if we embrace depression it can motivate us to change our lives for the better, helping us to learn from our mistakes and appreciate what we want. There is also research: one Dutch study suggested that people seemed to cope better with life's trials after depression, with improved averaged ratings of vitality, psychological health, social and leisure activities, occupational performance and general health. Meanwhile, a 2002 study from Duke University found that women who had had depression were more likely to live longer, fuelling speculation that the mildly depressed might learn to cope better and avoid harmful situations.

Other experts cautiously agree: "Depression can end in suicide, so it is not to be taken lightly," says Bridget O'Connell from Mind, "but many people say it helps them evaluate what is important. There is often a sense of 'I know I can survive', which gives self-belief and resilience." This can act as a wake-up call, encouraging people to change stressful patterns or situations. "They may find a job with shorter hours, or they may move in or out of cities."

According to Dr Paul Keedwell, a pyschiatrist and expert in mood disorders at Cardiff University, depression can do this by "taking off the optimistic sheen". In his book *How Sadness Survived* he argues that this has an evolutionary basis, as depression can benefit us by "putting the brakes on" and removing us from situations that cause chronic stress. "Though depression is horrible and no one would choose to go through it, it can help us be more realistic. And because it's so painful, we dig deeper and find out how not to go through it again." Antidepressants can help, adds Keedwell, "but if you carry on doing the same thing you did to get depressed, these antidepressants aren't going to work."

Tamra Mercieca, a performance coach and author of *The Upside of Down*, is one person who, after having suffered with depression all her life, which led to repeat suicide attempts, decided to make big life changes. These included stopping working shift work ("one of the major causes of depression"), seeing a life coach (to work through the negative thinking) and daily exercise (to boost endorphins). She also had weekly acupuncture and laughter clinics and made sure she was eating healthily and doing what she loved (in her case, writing and drumming).

She now says she feels thankful for her depression. "In overcoming the illness, I gained skills that have helped for other obstacles. I had

© Fran/Cartoonstock.com.

negative beliefs I needed to work through: I was a perfectionist and nothing I did was good enough, but now I have a very positive relationship with myself. Depression has helped me to help others. Seeing how effective neuro linguistic programming, time-line therapy and therapeutic hypnosis were in my recovery, I am now a performance coach, helping people overcome depression."

According to Wallace, many people who have experienced depression go on to be more empathetic. "It can also make them more aware of other dimensions to their lives which are not so reliant on everyday measures of failure and success."

Others, however, feel there are dangers in presenting depression in this way. Journalist Linda Jones, who regularly blogs on mental health (in Breaking the Silence), and has experienced depression herself ("a debilitating agony"), thinks that people may think it applies to everyone with depression "and that people with depression need to be more resilient, which plays into a stereotype that to suffer from depression you may be weak in the first place. I'm not and nor are millions of others, we have just been ill. Depression hasn't made my life better, it has made it worse. I am resilient, hardworking and focused anyway.

Laughing has been found to help relieve depression, a condition the author says is simply telling the depressed person something is wrong and needs changing.

When someone tells me this makes my life better, I question if they understand the depths I have fallen to."

Says Wallace: "Not everyone can feel any benefit from depression. It can depend on the length and severity, or some people may not respond to treatment. But there are others for whom it has been a turning point."

O'Connell agrees that we need to be careful in interpreting the research. "Some people self-report that they feel better after depression, but after a bad episode they are bound to say that in comparison to how low they felt during the illness." There is also the recurrence rate, which can be as high as 75 per cent for people who have had severe depression in the psychiatric service, but in general is much lower than that. "People may feel better for a while and then have another bout."

What all experts agree on is that getting good support is crucial to recovery: "The most important thing for recovery and future resilience is the support of family and friends," says O'Connell. And for anyone struggling with a loved one who is depressed? "Keep the communication open so they feel they can talk, but try to get support yourself as it is distressing watching someone you love struggle. There is a positive side, however. Most people do recover, most don't have recurrent episodes, and, anecdotally, many people say they emerge more resilient and able to take control of their lives."

EVALUATING THE AUTHOR'S ARGUMENTS:

Do you agree with the author, Rebecca Hardy that depression can in fact be good for you? Or, is depression bad for your long-term health, as the previous viewpoint by John Folk-Williams suggests? Support your answer by citing from both authors.

Depression Is the Main Cause of Teen Suicide

Gillian Graham

"Depression across all age groups is really the single largest underlying cause of suicide."

The following viewpoint presents an overview of the challenges facing families and individuals who must deal with teen suicide and contends that depression is the main reason teens end their lives. Gillian Graham tells the story of Haley Plaisted, a Maine teenager who committed suicide, leaving her family, friends, and community trying to understand what they could have done to help her. To answer these questions, Graham speaks to a variety of suicide experts who argue that while depression is to blame for most suicides in teens, carefully constructed and implemented state programs can provide an effective counter to this illness and its consequences. Graham is a staff writer for the *Morning Sentinel,* a central Maine newspaper.

AS YOU READ, CONSIDER THE FOLLOWING QUESTIONS:
1. According to suicide prevention expert Ann Haas, as cited by Graham, mental illness or substance abuse can be observed in what percentage of individuals who commit suicide?
2. What are the post-suicide services for the bereaved provided by the Maine Suicide Prevention Program, according to head of the Maine Suicide Prevention Program, as cited by the author?
3. The experts cited by the author identify what symptoms as prevalent in depressed teens who are at risk for committing suicide?

In the weeks since Haley Plaisted committed suicide, her family and friends have struggled to understand why the vibrant girl they knew wanted to end her life.

As they flip through photos of Plaisted with her arms around her sisters and riding on a dirt bike, they question if they could have done more to help her through the depression she rarely wanted to talk about. They wonder if bullying pushed her to the point she wanted to die, or if a break-up with her boyfriend was more than she could bear.

They have found no simple answers, a common situation facing those dealing with the complexities of suicide.

"I don't know how she got to that point," Plaisted's mother, Rebecca Liberty, said as she sat in her kitchen looking at photos of her youngest daughter. "She wasn't in her right mind. That child did not want to die."

Plaisted took her own life on April 8, [2012,] three days before her 17th birthday. It was a shock to her family—they say she never said she was thinking about suicide—but followed two years where Plaisted struggled with depression, bullying and a tumultuous relationship. She tried to kill herself for the first time in early 2012.

> **FAST FACT**
>
> The National Institute of Mental Health reports that more than 90 percent of people who die as a result of suicide suffered from depression or other mental disorder or a substance-abuse disorder, which often accompanies a mental disorder.

As emotional stories about teens who died by suicide grab headlines across the country, experts say people are starting to realize that communities need to have open conversations about suicide without fear it will prompt more people to take their own lives.

Teen Suicide Is a Complex Issue

At least three teens have committed suicide in Maine this year [2013], prompting both anti-suicide and anti-bullying vigils and educational sessions for students, teachers and administrators grappling with how to deal with the shock and grief that follow suicide deaths. Gov. Paul LePage recently signed a law that requires the Department of Education to adopt standards for suicide prevention and education training in schools.

But while it is important to talk about suicide causes and prevention, experts say much of the recent media coverage that blames suicide solely on bullying oversimplifies an issue that is far more complex.

"The bullying discussion has had an effect on bringing suicide out into a more open place where it can be talked about," said Ann Haas, senior director of education and prevention for the American Foundation of Suicide Prevention. However, she said, "I think much of the discussion has not been helpful because it has created a narrative in the public mind that youth suicide is a byproduct of bullying."

Maine has a higher rate of youth suicide than the national average and the highest rate in the Northeast, according to the Centers for Disease Control and Prevention.

From 2005 to 2009, there were 901 suicides in Maine, of which 93 were committed by people younger than 24. Suicide is the second leading cause of death among Mainers aged 15 to 34. On average, there is one suicide every two days in Maine.

Greg Marley, who oversees the Maine Suicide Prevention Program, said youth suicide rates peaked in the late 1990s, after a decades-long increase. After the peak, suicide rates remained relatively flat until around 2005, when rates in both Maine and across the country started to rise again.

Marley said it is hard to determine why there has been an increase across the country, but said rural states like Maine generally have higher suicide rates than urban areas. That is because people tend to be more isolated from social support and professional intervention, have easier access to guns and live in a culture where fewer people seek treatment for mental illness, he said.

In recent months, youth suicide in Maine and across the country has become more public as families speak out about teens they say committed suicide because of bullying or after forced sexual encounters. While those external factors can contribute to feelings of depression or hopelessness, experts say the cause of suicide is often more complex than the headlines reveal and that addressing the issue can be both delicate and challenging.

"We work hard to dispel the notion that suicide happens because of bad life events," Haas said. "Depression across all age groups is really the single largest underlying cause of suicide."

Research shows that 90 percent of those who commit suicide have a mental illness or substance abuse issue, Haas said.

While the reasons people kill themselves can be complex and hard to understand, so too are the conversations about suicide that need to happen to prevent more deaths, experts say. Haas said the stigma of talking about suicide is slowly dissipating, but it's still an issue that isn't discussed enough.

"When you're talking about suicide, it opens the door to allow someone to talk about the stress they're feeling," Marley said. "If it's shameful or looked at as being negative, people hide it in the closet."

Haley Plaisted's family and friends know they cannot undo what she did, but they hope to bring more attention to suicide prevention and bullying by talking about her. Her cousin, Craig Bartlett, organized a vigil at a Sanford [Maine] park to try to start a conversation in the community about how to prevent suicide. That type of action has come as a comfort to some of Plaisted's friends.

"I hope people realize suicide should never be an option," said Kailie Page, a friend. "Everyone has something to live for."

Depression Is Not Always Visible

Those closest to Plaisted remember her as an upbeat, fun and intensely loyal friend who was always trying to make people laugh. She grew up in rural York County, the daughter of Rebecca Liberty and Shane Plaisted.

One minute she'd be racing through the neighborhood on a dirt bike and the next she'd be dressing herself up in girly clothes. She

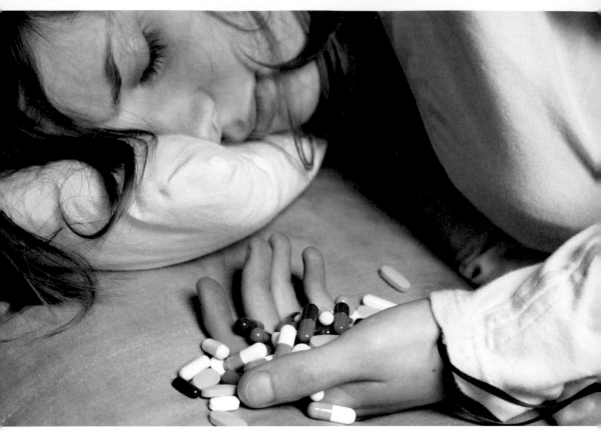

Numerous experts agree that serious depression can lead to suicide, especially in teens.

was always trying to help other people and make them happy, but sometimes her good intentions were misunderstood, her family said.

"She just wanted to be going, going, going," Liberty said of her daughter. "She was something else."

While she often put on a happy front, Plaisted had been struggling with depression and bullying in the past few years, her mother said. She occasionally told her family she was feeling depressed, but never really wanted to talk about it. By 15, she was taking mood stabilizers prescribed to help her deal with depression.

After a physical encounter with a girl who threatened her at Massabesic High School, Plaisted transferred to Sanford [High School], Liberty said. She was also bullied there and withdrew from school earlier this year to get away from it, Liberty said.

A little more than a year ago, Plaisted attempted suicide. The attempt came months after her mother's husband died of cancer and Haley broke up with a serious boyfriend. She stayed briefly at Spring Harbor [Hospital] and moved out of state for a time to stay with her older sister. Her family thought a fresh start would be good for Plaisted, but she never wanted to be far away from her mother and friends.

Whenever her daughter was upset, Liberty said, she would try to talk to her about it.

"She would clam up. She was thinking pills were going to make her feel better," Liberty said. "She never wanted people to help her."

Instead, Liberty said, Plaisted seemed focused on finding love and creating a family of her own.

"Haley was looking for love. When she loved somebody, she didn't love them just a tiny bit, she loved them tons and tons and tons," she said. "She didn't know so many people loved her so much. It was like she couldn't believe someone did love her that much."

Plaisted's friends would sometimes catch a glimpse of her stress and anxiety, but more often she was singing goofy songs or looking for an adventure.

"She lit up the world in a way nobody else could," said family friend Jayde Burgess. "But she had a lot of pain most people couldn't deal with for that long."

Page, the 14-year-old friend from Sanford, grew up with Plaisted but said her friend never opened up about depression.

"I knew she had a lot of pain, but she never came to me. I couldn't help her," Page said moments after releasing balloons into the air on the day Plaisted would have turned 17. "She really was a lost person."

Suicide Can Be Unexpected

At the balloon release, Liberty clutched a portrait of her daughter as she watched butterfly balloons disappear into the sky. Afterward, family and friends huddled together to talk about Plaisted, their stories punctuated by both laughter and tears.

Alan Cyr, whom Plaisted considered to be her stepfather even though he and her mother divorced years ago, said she seemed to transform from a happy kid to a troubled teenager, but it was tough to tell if she was just rebelling or if something deeper was going on. She started keeping more of a distance from her family—especially her parents—and would take off from home to avoid fighting with her mom about drinking and swearing.

Cyr said Plaisted seemed to be searching for acceptance from everyone around her.

"It was like taking a square peg and putting her in a round hole. She wasn't going to fit into the round hole the world wanted her to," he said. "She was trying really hard to reach this level of acceptance I didn't think she was going to get from people."

In the weeks before she died, Plaisted was couch-surfing [spending the night] at friends' houses. Her mother received only the occasional text from Plaisted and had no idea if her daughter was taking her medication properly or at all.

"She was bouncing around. She was so confused," Liberty said. "She wanted to be an adult and make her own life."

In those weeks, Plaisted posted frequently on her Facebook page, sometimes about drinking and drug use. Her posts show a range of emotion, from excitement about her birthday and hanging out with friends to sadness about the breakup of her relationship. Her friends say photos Plaisted posted of herself in a bikini prompted taunts from peers who often picked on her.

"Sooner or later I'm not gonna have a heart cause it's been hurt so much it won't be able to be put together," Plaisted wrote in one Facebook post.

After weeks away, Plaisted finally came home on a Sunday night.

Her older sister was in town and Plaisted wanted to see her young niece. Plaisted's family knew she had just broken up with the boyfriend she thought she would marry. But they didn't suspect she was considering suicide.

Liberty said her daughter's face was puffy from crying, but she brightened up when they talked about her upcoming birthday and she made plans to hang out with a friend. When her mother went to bed that night, Plaisted was exchanging text messages with her ex-boyfriend, Liberty said.

The next morning, Liberty found her daughter's body in the garage: She had hanged herself sometime after her family went to bed for the night. The family doesn't know if Plaisted left a note on her iPod, which was taken by police as part of the investigation.

"She was home, I didn't think . . . ," Liberty said, her voice trailing off as she was overcome with emotion. "I had all sorts of things I wanted to do with her. That morning I wanted to snuggle with her and talk about what to do (for her birthday). It was too late."

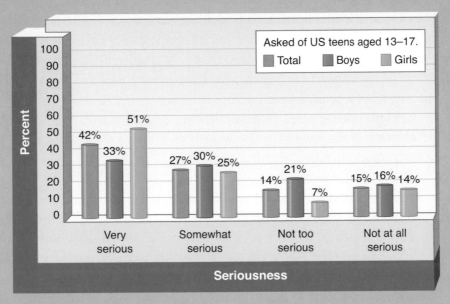

How serious a problem do you think each of the following health issues is among your teenaged friends regarding depression and suicide?

Taken from: Coleen McMurray. "Nearly Half of Teens Aware of Peer Suicide Attempts." Gallup, May 25, 2004. www.gallup.com.

Amber Killer McCormick, Plaisted's older sister, said the family is still trying to make sense of what happened.

"We thought she was safe," she said. "She was home."

Suicide Prevention Programs Are Necessary to Save Lives

Marley, who oversees the Maine Suicide Prevention Program, said Maine has been seen as a leader in developing training, outreach and support around youth suicide.

The prevention program was launched in 1998 when then-Gov. Angus King recognized the rate of youth suicide in Maine was significantly higher than the national average.

By 2010, the focus of the program had shifted from helping young people to preventing suicide among Mainers of all ages. Much of the work revolves around providing education and training programs in schools and to groups of adults.

Last week [late May 2013], LePage signed L.D. 609, a bipartisan bill to increase suicide awareness and prevention in public schools. The bill requires the Department of Education to adopt rules on standards for schools for prevention education and training. The training and education will include suicide prevention awareness education for all personnel. At least two people in each school district will be required to take more advanced suicide prevention and intervention training. LePage pledged $44,000 from his contingency fund to support implementation of the bill. Schools must train staff by the end of the 2015–16 school year.

"The devastating effect suicide has on Maine families and communities is real, and we must be willing to address the issue," LePage said in a statement after signing the bill.

After a school or community experiences a suicide death, the Maine Suicide Prevention Program is able to come in to provide information, resources and guidance to help people through the shock and grief. All schools are required to have a crisis team in place to deal with those types of situations, but how prepared they are to deal specifically with a suicide death "varies considerably," Marley said.

Marley said that kind of post-suicide response—or "postvention"—is helpful because it helps address immediate needs, but also lowers the risk of copycat or associated suicides. The risk of suicide contagion is most prevalent among youth and young adults.

"Good postvention is good suicide prevention," he said.

The program's goals now include focusing on suicide prevention among working-age adults and integrating suicide prevention into the primary health care provider setting. Marley said involving primary care doctors in suicide prevention is important because it provides an opportunity to identify people who are struggling.

"People are still reluctant, particularly adults, to reach out for anything labeled mental health help," he said.

A Conversation About Teen Depression Must Be Started

Haas, from the national suicide prevention group, said one of the most important aspects of suicide prevention efforts—including those in Maine—is the focus on how to recognize depression and help people who are struggling. While experts know most people who commit suicide have a mental illness such as depression, symptoms can be harder to recognize in teens than adults.

"It often isn't the kind of sadness and teariness that most people think of with depression," Haas said. "(Depression in youth) can be angry, oppositional behavior, drinking and other kinds of acting out."

Teens with depression can be argumentative and unpleasant, which "makes it harder to keep the focus on the child and what they need, because it seems like behavioral problems," Haas said.

The American Foundation for Suicide Prevention created films about depression in teens to show at schools and to adults, which she said have been effective in starting conversations and educating people about the problem.

"We need to do a lot more educating about the role of depression. It is treatable," Haas said. "The really difficult part about it is it doesn't mean it always prevents suicide. It's not a guarantee that we can get a young person on a different course, but treatment is the best course."

Marley of the Maine Suicide Prevention Program agrees.

"The majority of young people who attempt suicide and get the help they need go on to not get back into another suicide crisis again." That's why, Marley said, it's so important to make sure "if someone is feeling suicidal or considering making an attempt on their life, they get serious intervention help to move beyond that place where their life isn't working."

EVALUATING THE AUTHOR'S ARGUMENTS:

Depression is identified in this viewpoint by Gillian Graham as the leading cause of suicide. After reading this viewpoint, think about what you have heard in the news about teen suicide recently and everything else you have read in this chapter. Do you believe that depression is the leading cause, or do you think there are there other, more important factors to consider? Use specific examples from the articles or outside readings to support your answer.

Chapter 2

What Are the Causes of Depression?

A poor diet has been found to contribute to depression in some people.

A Genetic Link to Depression Exists

NHS Choices

"[There is] 'clear evidence' that a region on chromosome 3 . . . is linked to severe recurrent depression."

In the following viewpoint NHS Choices, the website of the British National Health Service, reports on a study conducted by researchers from the Institute of Psychiatry at King's College, London, and other research centers throughout Europe and North America. The study found a genetic link for severe, recurring depression. NHS Choices explains that the study involved the comparing of 971 pairs of siblings who had histories of severe, recurrent depression, as well as other family members from 839 European families. The researchers reportedly found "clear evidence" of markers for severe, recurrent depression on chromosome 3 of the subjects. The viewpoint notes that both genetic and environmental factors contribute to depression but that genetics seem to play a larger role in severe, recurrent depression.

AS YOU READ, CONSIDER THE FOLLOWING QUESTIONS:
  1. What was the region on chromosome 3 where the link was found called, according to NHS Choices?
  2. As noted by the author, what might the study not apply to?
  3. According to the author's report, what does the study appear to give to the genetic contribution to depression?

"Scientists have for the first time established a genetic cause for depression narrowing it down to a specific chromosome," reports *The Independent*. It said that the study has found "clear evidence" that a region on chromosome 3 (called 3p25-26) is linked to severe recurrent depression.

This study looked at DNA from 971 sibling pairs who have European ancestry and who are affected by recurrent depression. Its findings are supported by another study published at the same time that found a link between the same region of chromosome 3 and depression in a sample of families of heavy smokers. This was reported to be the first time such a link had been independently confirmed in two studies.

One point worth noting is that these results may not apply to less severe, non-recurrent depression, or to individuals of non-European ancestry, who were not included in this study. Also, this finding does not mean that this is the only region containing genes that contribute to depression.

The study was not able to pinpoint single letter variations in the regions that were linked to severe recurrent depression, and the gene(s) involved have yet to be identified. Future work is likely to focus on studying the genes within the region, to identify which ones may be having an effect.

The study was carried out by researchers from the Institute of Psychiatry at King's College, London, and many other research centres in Europe and North America. Some of the researchers worked for GlaxoSmithKline, who also provided funding for recruiting participants and collecting DNA samples. The study was published in the peer-reviewed *American Journal of Psychiatry*.

This story was covered by *The Independent, Daily Mail, Financial Times* and the *Daily Mirror. The Independent* and *Financial Times* provided balanced coverage, with *The Independent* noting the region identified may only contribute a small amount to a person's susceptibility to depression. The *Financial Times* noted that many genes are likely to play a role. The *Daily Mail* suggested that 'depression could be caused by a single rogue gene' but this is not likely to be the case.

Family Patterns of Depression Were Studied

This was a 'genome wide linkage study', called the Depression Network Study, which aimed to identify areas of DNA that might contain genes contributing to a person's susceptibility to major depression. Both genetic and environmental factors are thought to play a role in the development of disorders such as depression. Studies have

At least one study has found "clear evidence" that a region on chromosome 3 (called 3p25-26) is linked to severe recurrent depression.

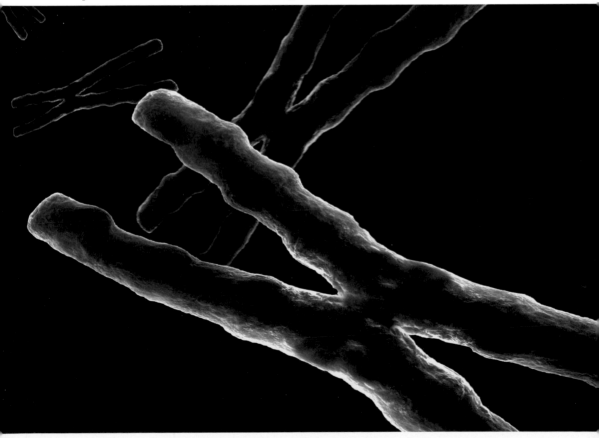

suggested that genetics play a greater role in depression that is severe and recurrent than in less severe, non-recurrent depression.

This type of study looks at DNA inheritance patterns within families that include sibling pairs affected by the disease in question. They use identifiable variations within the DNA called 'markers' to find pieces of DNA that are consistently passed on to the affected sibling pairs. Once such a region is identified the researchers look at the genes within that region in more detail, to see if they could be contributing to the disease.

This method is commonly used in looking for genes that cause diseases.

The researchers enrolled 839 families, which included 971 pairs of siblings who had recurrent major depression, the families also included 118 pairs where one sibling was affected but not the other, and 12 unaffected sibling pairs.

Adult siblings of European ancestry were recruited from eight sites across Europe and the UK. Sibling pairs were excluded if either sibling had ever had mania (bipolar), hypomania, schizophrenia or psychotic symptoms, or had intravenous drug dependency or depression associated with alcohol use. To be eligible, both siblings had to have experienced at least two depressive episodes of at least moderate severity, with the episodes separated by at least two months of remission, according to accepted criteria.

As well as the sibling pairs, the study recruited additional siblings and parents if they were available. All participants were interviewed using a standard clinical interview to assess the presence of psychiatric diagnoses. The interview also asked participants to rate the presence and severity of various symptoms during the worst four to six weeks of their worst and second worst episodes of depression. This information was used to categorise the severity of a person's depression.

In total, 2,412 people were included: 2,164 of these had recurrent depression, 1,447 were classified as having severe or worse recurrent depression, and 827 with very severe recurrent depression.

Participants provided a blood sample for DNA extraction and their DNA was assessed for 1,130 genetic markers spread across the chromosomes. Statistical programmes were then used to analyse the results to identify regions of DNA that showed a pattern of inheritance consistent with the possibility that a gene contributing to the development of depression was nearby.

The researchers carried out separate analyses for the overall sample with recurrent depression, for severe recurrent depression and very severe recurrent depression.

Once the researchers identified a region of DNA that showed linkage to recurrent depression, they aimed to test these results using a case control analysis of a sample of 2,960 individuals with recurrent depression (cases) and 1,594 healthy individuals (controls). The cases came from the current study, as well as 1,346 individuals with recurrent depression from another study of depression in the UK. The controls were from the UK Medical Research Council general practice research framework, and staff and student volunteers from King's College London. Using DNA samples from these individuals, the researchers looked at 1,878 single 'letter' variations in the region identified as being linked to recurrent depression in the first part of the study.

Early Results Show a Genetic Link to Depression

The researchers identified a region on the short arm of chromosome 3 (called 3p25-26) that was linked to severe recurrent depression. Importantly, this link remained significant after the researchers took into account the fact that many markers had been tested for linkage. There were 214 genes within the region of chromosome 3 identified as being linked to severe recurrent depression. Based on what is known about the proteins that these genes encode a number of these genes that seemed like strong potential candidates for being involved in depression, for example, some of the genes in the region encoded the receptors for various brain signaling chemicals.

Some other regions showed weaker signs of linkage to recurrent depression as a whole, or very severe recurrent depression, but only the region on chromosome 3 was investigated further as it showed the strongest linkage.

Because the linkage with the region on chromosome 3 was greatest in sibling pairs with severe recurrent depression, in their case-control analysis the researchers only analysed the 1,590 cases with severe recurrent depression, and 1,589 controls. The researchers found that 95 single letter genetic variations showed some evidence of an association with the cases. However, these associations lost their significance once the many statistical tests that were carried out were taken into account. They say that this lack of significant findings may be because there are multiple rare variations having an effect, or that their sample may not have been large enough to detect common variants each having a mild effect.

In their discussion, the researchers highlight another study published in the same journal, which has also found linkage with the same region of chromosome 3 in a sample of families of heavy smokers with depression.

The researchers conclude that they have identified a region of chromosome 3 that shows linkage to recurrent depression. They say that this region includes genes that could plausibly be involved in this condition.

The researchers added that this is the first report of a region showing linkage to depression from a genome-wide study, which has then been supported by findings from an independent sample. They say that future work will involve determining the DNA sequence of this region in the affected siblings and their families, and assessing the region in other samples with severe recurrent depression.

Genetic and Environmental Factors Play a Role

Depression is thought to involve both genetic and environmental factors, with genetics playing a larger role in the type of depression that is severe and recurrent. This study has identified a region of DNA that may include a gene or genes that affect an individual's susceptibility to severe recurrent depression.

One point worth noting is that these results may not apply to less severe, non-recurrent depression, or to individuals of non-European ancestry, who were not included in this study. Also, the regions iden-

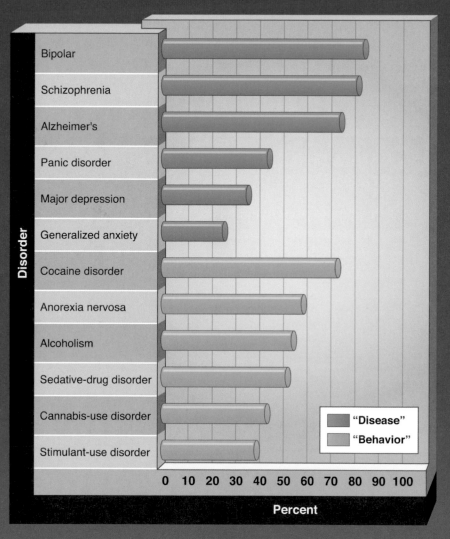

Inheritance of Disease and Behavior in Twins

The graph shows the rate at which various behavioral disorders, such as depression, are heritable.

Disorder

- Bipolar
- Schizophrenia
- Alzheimer's
- Panic disorder
- Major depression
- Generalized anxiety
- Cocaine disorder
- Anorexia nervosa
- Alcoholism
- Sedative-drug disorder
- Cannabis-use disorder
- Stimulant-use disorder

"Disease"
"Behavior"

0 10 20 30 40 50 60 70 80 90 100

Percent

Taken from: Teejay Anthony Santos. "Young Adult Depression: Role of Genetics." depression-genetics-wikispaces.com.

tified in this study are unlikely to be the only ones containing genes that contribute to depression.

The authors have been appropriately circumspect with regard to their findings, noting that it is still possible these results are false positives, and their statistical results suggest there is a 1.5% chance this is the case. They say their results need replication in other studies, and for the genes actually responsible for this link to be identified. The fact that another study published concurrently has also found a link with the same region of chromosome 3 lends support to the findings but, ideally, further confirmation in other samples will be obtained.

This study appears to give an important clue to the genetic contribution to severe recurrent depression, and future work is likely to focus on studying the genes within the region, to identify which one(s) may be contributing.

EVALUATING THE AUTHOR'S ARGUMENTS:

NHS Choices presents detailed results of the study connecting depression to a genetic marker. Are you satisfied with the article's conclusion on a genetic link to depression, or do you think the environment and circumstance plays a larger role in depression? If you think environment and circumstance are greater factors, give an example to support your view.

There Is No Genetic Link to Depression

Anne Buchanan

"A massive effort to uncover genes involved in depression has largely failed."

Anne Buchanan, a senior research associate at Penn State University, argues in the following viewpoint that a genetic cause for depression has not been found, following a massive study on the subject, because life is so complex. Buchanan analyzes the study carefully and concludes that its authors' inability to find conclusive answers to the origins of depression is similar to other studies on equally complicated traits and illnesses. These findings lead Buchanan to believe that the study's authors failed to find the genetic link because no single genetic cause for depression exists, confirming that varied factors contribute to the development of individual characteristics and diseases.

AS YOU READ, CONSIDER THE FOLLOWING QUESTIONS:
1. What percentage of depression is genetically caused, according to the study cited by the author?
2. What does Buchanan identify as the problem with increasing the study to include fifty thousand cases?
3. As stated by the author, what have scientists known for ninety-four years about traits seen within families?

D epression seems to run in families, but despite numerous attempts, few causal genes have been identified and even fewer have been replicated. Why?

Twin and family studies have estimated heritability, or the proportion of the cause of depression that is genetic, to be 31–42%, according to a newly published report in *Biological Psychiatry*. This is a report of a meta-analysis that pooled results from 17 genomewide association studies (GWAS), including a total of 34,549 people of European origin with depression somewhere along a continuum defined by the answers to 20 questions as to extent of depressed mood, feelings of guilt and worthlessness, feelings of helplessness and hopelessness, psychomotor retardation, loss of appetite, and sleep disturbance. This study differs from most others in that it used symptoms rather than diagnosis.

They also attempted to replicate their findings with 5 studies that used a different assessment of depressive symptoms, the requirement these days for validating a study. Finally, they did a combined meta-analysis of a number of discovery and replication studies, for a total of 51,258 individuals.

The Search for a Depression Gene
Summed up bluntly by *Science News*:

> A massive effort to uncover genes involved in depression has largely failed. By combing through the DNA of 34,549 volunteers, an international team of 86 scientists hoped to uncover genetic influences that affect a person's vulnerability to depression. But the analysis turned up nothing.

Well, not exactly nothing. The authors report one hit when they pooled all the studies, but it did not replicate any other studies, and it was in a genomic region that included no genes. That's not necessarily meaningless, but it is difficult to follow up.

The authors wonder whether using the depression scale might explain this lack of hits. Were their cases so heterogeneous [diverse] that this prevented them from finding a major effect? If they'd included only people who scored high on the scale, perhaps this would have narrowed down possible causal genes, or eliminated cases of depression that might not have a genetic basis. The authors wrote:

The approach of studying depression on a continuum has the advantage that not only information on extremes is used but that all available information is exploited. [Researcher Sophie] Van der Sluis et al. showed that if the phenotypic variation among cases, as well as the variation among control subjects, is used, this greatly increases the power to detect genetic variants.

But, given that no other study has replicably found genes with major effect, it is unlikely that this explains the lack of significant findings. Their replication studies may have added a different phenotype [observable trait] to the mix, too, and therefore additional genetic heterogeneity. The authors also point out that gene-gene interaction or gene-environment interactions might explain depression, and hinder GWAS.

By combing through the DNA of 34,549 volunteers, an international team of eighty-six scientists hoped to uncover genetic traits that affect a person's vulnerability to depression.

© Fran/Cartoonstock.com.

Of course, the authors (naturally, and with total scientific disinterestedness) say that the way to do this right is to do a larger study of, say, 50,000 cases. But of course this won't eliminate any of the issues, and will only increase the heterogeneity problem.

Genetic Inheritance Can Be Difficult to Determine

Showing that this isn't just evidence of sloppy workmanship is the fact that similar results have been found for most other psychiatric or neurological disorders, with few exceptions, and that even 'mechanical' traits like the skeleton, metabolism, and so on, that are easier to define and measure show the same level of complexity. Even in yeast.

Is it fair to point out that we have known for a mere 94 years that it is absolutely consistent that traits without major genetic contributions can cluster in families, so that substantial heritability is not an indicator that mapping will find such genes. While families with many cases in many generations and collateral relatives (like cousins) do raise hopes of such effects at least in those families, it was long ago also shown that polygenic causation [caused by multiple genes] (which is what we have here, if the evidence is to be believed) can mimic Mendelian transmission [caused by a single gene] families.

So this study, like so many costly others, tells us what we knew. Indeed, we already knew we knew that before this (and so many other) study was done.

The Absence of an Answer Confirms Life's Complexity

We're in the age in which we boast about our various name-dropping technologies that we used in our latest elephantine [enormous] study. We make sure our listeners know that we've used 'massively parallel' or 'Next-generation' sequencing to get data from massive numbers of people. The idea is that signal-to-noise ratios are well-behaved, so that increasing sample sizes will find increasingly weaker signals [that is, the larger the sample, the clearer the results].

There is no reason to believe this, when it comes to genetics, and indeed there are good reasons to think the contrary. But that doesn't slow down the current *modus operandi* [way of doing things]: generating *massively incremental* data.

Actually, on the other hand, the 'nothing' that is being found is nothing to be depressed about! Instead, it's convincing evidence for complexity—that is, that many minor causes interact and combine to generate results, so that each case is different in detail, both in terms of the trait itself and the genotype [nonobservable, gene-level traits] that contributes to it. It's the nothing we don't want because what we want is something we can cash in on: build a career as the discoverer of the Big Fact, make and profit from a patent, make a pharmaceutical bonanza.

> **FAST FACT**
>
> A *Science News* article in January 2013 reported that a large-scale, international scientific study conducted by eighty-six scientists using nearly thirty-five thousand volunteers failed to discover any gene that could be said to cause depression.

Instead, it's the mouse that roared [that is, much ado about nothing]. We should be taking credit for showing how life really seems to be, which all these GWAS have in fact shown, but few are willing to accept it. Of course, we needn't do that thousands of times, except that that's what we're doing because of the paucity of better ideas. But that's how humans, at least humans in our kind of culture, seem to operate.

> ## EVALUATING THE AUTHOR'S ARGUMENTS:
>
> In this viewpoint Anne Buchanan makes the argument that scientific studies have confirmed that illnesses like depression that seem to be genetically caused and inherited do not actually have a single gene that controls them. How does this impact your understanding of depression? Do you believe that the lack of a genetic link changes the way that individuals should respond to and treat depression? Explain.

Junk Food Can Cause Depression

"Those who ate greater amounts of processed foods . . . were more likely to develop depressive symptoms than those who ate more natural, whole foods."

Caitlin Covington

While conceding that there is no proven causal relationship between any type of food and depression, Caitlin Covington argues in the following viewpoint that research has shown that diet can impact one's mood, both positively and negatively. Covington cites numerous studies confirming that foods high in fats have been linked to several symptoms common to depression. In contrast, she points to research suggesting that eating foods high in B vitamins, Omega-3s, and complex carbohydrates may actually improve an individual's mood and counter depression's debilitating side effects. In light of these findings, she urges individuals to make informed dietary choices to change their mood. Covington is a college student and contributor to the health and wellness website Greatist.

AS YOU READ, CONSIDER THE FOLLOWING QUESTIONS:
1. What types of fats have been connected to depression, according to research cited by the author?
2. As stated by Covington, what are the possible effects of diets low in protein and fatty acids?
3. What does the author identify as the benefit of eating complex carbohydrates?

S ure, eating a tub of ice cream may cause some tears of guilt afterwards, but there are no specific foods that are proven to cause depression. Instead, research suggests certain eating patterns might be associated with symptoms like sadness and anxiety.

Specifically, diets low in B vitamins and Omega-3 fatty acids and high in saturated fat and trans fats (yep—even those beloved potato chips!) may be linked to depression.

Many Dietary Choices Can Increase the Risk for Depression

French fries and Twinkies may taste delish, but there's a reason to beware [of] eating too much saturated fat and trans fat (even besides high cholesterol and a higher risk of coronary heart disease). Research has linked depression to a diet high in saturated fats (found in animal-based foods such as meat, milk, and cheese) and trans fats otherwise known as partially hydrogenated oils. In one six-year study researchers [in Spain working on the SUN project] found people who ate more trans fats were at greater risk for depression than those who consumed smaller amounts of the terrible T's. It turns out trans fats may increase the risk for feeling down in the dumps because they cause inflammation in the heart

> **FAST FACT**
>
> Researchers in Spain report that results from their 2012 study suggest that people who eat lots of fast food are 37 percent more likely to suffer from depression than are those who do not eat a lot of fast food.

and brain. And although it's not clear whether inflammation directly causes depression, studies have found depressed patients show higher levels of inflammation than other people.

But don't blame it all on the potato chips! Research suggests certain nutritional deficiencies may also contribute to symptoms of depression. Another study [in the *British Journal of Psychiatry*] followed middle-aged adults for five years and found those who ate greater amounts of processed foods (like processed meat, sweet desserts, fried food, and refined cereals) were more likely to develop depressive symptoms than those who ate more natural, whole foods (like vegetables, fruits, and fish).

Scientists suspect the crowd who prefers sweet treats over fruits and veggies are skimping on antioxidants, which may protect against depression. They may also be missing out on whole foods rich in folate, a nutrient that protects neurotransmitters in the brain, since patients with depression have about 25 percent lower folate levels than healthy adults. And a hardcore sweat session may not be the only reason to chug some protein: It's also possible that diets lacking in protein and fatty acids can cause nervous system dysfunction and increase the risk for depression. On the other hand, scientists can't say for sure that eating doughnuts for dinner is the culprit behind anyone's mental health issues.

Junk foods such as Twinkies and French fries contain trans fats, which negatively affect physical health and in some cases worsen depression.

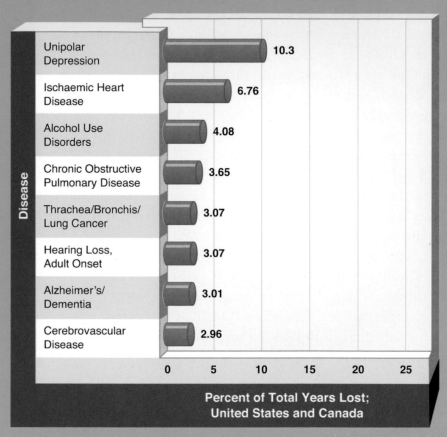

Years of Life Lost to Disease in the United States and Canada

Disease	Percent of Total Years Lost
Unipolar Depression	10.3
Ischaemic Heart Disease	6.76
Alcohol Use Disorders	4.08
Chronic Obstructive Pulmonary Disease	3.65
Thrachea/Bronchis/Lung Cancer	3.07
Hearing Loss, Adult Onset	3.07
Alzheimer's/Dementia	3.01
Cerebrovascular Disease	2.96

Percent of Total Years Lost; United States and Canada

Taken from: National Institute of Mental Health. "Leading Causes of Diseases/Disorders." Data Courtesy of World Health Organization.

A Change in Diet Could Combat Depression

Depression and nutrition is a chicken-and-egg kinda' deal—it's hard to know whether depression causes unhealthy eating or unhealthy eating results in depression. Research suggests depressed people tend to get caught in a cycle and continue to make poor food choices that may worsen their symptoms.

But there may be a reason to rejoice after all—although there's no certifiable food cure for depression, eating a varied diet may help banish the blues. Noshing on the following foods could help prevent depression:

- *B vitamins.* These nutrients are essential for a happy, healthy body, and foods rich in vitamin B12 can help balance the chemicals in the brain. To get a daily dose, chow down on organ meats (such as beef liver or turkey giblets) and fortified cereals. Folate (another B vitamin) also helps produce and maintain new cells, so ward off low spirits with natural folate found in dark green leafy vegetables, dried beans, and citrus juices.

- *Omega-3s.* Incorporating omega-3 fatty acids into a healthy diet can help reduce symptoms of depression and anxiety. Get fishing—the main sources of omega fatty acids are found in fish, such as herring, rainbow trout, salmon, and tuna. For those who aren't fans of seafood, get a fatty acid fix from flaxseed, soybeans, walnuts, and canola oil.

- *Complex Carbohydrates.* Load up on carbs! (Yep, we said it.) Carbohydrate-rich foods trigger the production of the neurotransmitter serotonin which regulates mood. Look for complex carbs, rather than sweets, to provide a lasting effect on brain chemistry and mood.

If serious depression is an issue, consider seeing a therapist to find a personal treatment plan. Otherwise aim for a balanced, varied diet with plenty of natural, whole foods. The health benefits of proper nutrition are just another reason to smile.

EVALUATING THE AUTHOR'S ARGUMENTS:

The author of this article, Caitlin Covington, makes a number of claims regarding the benefits and consequences of eating a variety of foods. Do you think she provides sufficient evidence to support her claims? Why or why not? Can you offer any evidence from your own experience to show that eating certain foods impacts your mood? Use specific examples in your answer.

Dieting Can Cause Depression

Rebecca Jane Stokes

"Changing your diet drastically— restricting fat and sugar— actually creates symptoms of withdrawal, which affect your dopamine levels, making you edgy, emotional, and angry."

In the viewpoint that follows Rebecca Jane Stokes uses her own experiences to describe the perils of dieting and its nega- tive effects on one's mood and well-being. She recounts how dieting always left her feeling empty, both literally and figurative- ly, and never led her to the happiness she desired. Stokes supports her personal story with evidence from research showing that strict dieting can lead to the same symp- toms of withdrawal experienced by drug addicts. The author concludes that to beat the symptoms of depression associated with dieting, she had to realize that hap- piness is not connected to weight. Stokes is a writer and humorist who contributes regularly to *xoJane,* an online women's magazine.

Rebecca Jane Stokes, "Science Says Dieting Causes Depression and I Am So Not Surprised," *xoJane,* December 17, 2012. Originally published on www.xojane.com. Reprinted with permission of Say Media Inc.

A lot of things bum me out—vending machines accepting exact change only; bras whose underwire gives up the ghost too soon, but not before stabbing my tender pit-meats; walking into leftover fart in a revolving door—but nothing bums me out the way dieting does.

Sure, there can be the initial flutter of excitement that comes with buying the new permissible food, getting the hang of the new routine—be it recording the calories, the points, the carbs. But when the novelty ebbs, it leaves inside me a feeling of leaden unhappiness. Also hunger.

The Dieting Cycle Is Difficult to Stop

I've dieted, in one form or another, since I was 12. I don't remember ever thinking my body was OK. I went from not thinking about it at all to running to my mother, tears in my eyes, at the development of the livid red stretch mark etching my inner thighs. It can't be easy to be a mom, and being a mom to a little girl and watching her struggle and fail to accept herself, mimicking your own patterns in relation to food and her body as my mother had to do, must be a special brand of heartbreaking.

I went to a nutritionist before I was a teenager. I stepped onto the accommodating scale and stared down at my belly, ignoring the flashing red number. Just two rolls, I thought, I have just two rolls, that's not so bad, I can get rid of two rolls. I watched my friends leave half-eaten cookies, thinking, "How can they do that?" To me, unfinished confection remains one of life's greatest mysteries.

I joined the swim team because at the end of the week I could reward myself with a package of Now and Laters [candy]. I made the snacks and foods I enjoyed rewards for physical activity, putting everything from chocolate bars to mashed potatoes on a pedestal. I counted calories and stepped onto the Stairmaster with whatever book I was reading.

I'd think about how when I was skinny, everything would be different. I lost weight and gained weight and lost weight and gained weight, but any change in my life that happened didn't coincide with there being less of me. I continued climbing imaginary stairs, directing montages about a big romance and a skinny me set to the music of Alanis Morissette. So in other words, I continued to bork [screw up] my relationships with food, my body and reality.

Even as the pounds came off my still-developing body, I was unhappy. [An] article [on the *Science Daily* website from December 12, 2012,] discusses how changing your diet drastically—restricting fat and sugar—actually creates symptoms of withdrawal, which affect your dopamine levels, making you edgy, emotional, and angry. You know, LIKE A DRUG ADDICT. It's a parallel people have made before—and while the similarities are there, here's the big difference: you need food to live. There is no telling yourself that once you get through withdrawal it will be the last time—you have to eat food forever.

So in addition to contending with my self-worth issues, and the complex societal messaging branded into my tiny brain at so young an age, I was actually making shit even harder for myself, perpetuating a cycle that ensured total, permanent misery. Ashamed Becca, Happy Becca, Dieting Becca, Giving Up Becca, Happy Becca, Ashamed Becca, Dieting Becca—it is like a carousel where they give you free funnel cake and then speed shit up until it's so out of hand that the free funnel cake makes a second appearance. I call this the carousel of suck.

> **FAST FACT**
>
> NHS Choices, the British National Health Service information center, suggests that studies linking fast food to depression fail to account for the fact that the condition of depression and the high levels of fast-food consumption may both result from other factors, such as being single or being less active.

Acceptance, Not Dieting, Leads to Happiness

It didn't occur to me that my unhappiness might not rest with how I looked, but in how I was living until—this July?

But it's not like it was an overnight revelation—it was 17 years of restriction, self-castigation and shaaaame. I think the biggest myth about dieting is that when you achieve whatever pound-goal you have set in your head, your life will have changed for the better. To be smaller, to reduce yourself means you'll be able to attract the sort of romantic partner you want, you'll get the sort of job you deserve, you'll just be more innately happy.

But the thing is, that's hokum. The thing you get when you lose weight is a different number on a scale. That number isn't good or bad. That number has no real power at all other than what we assign

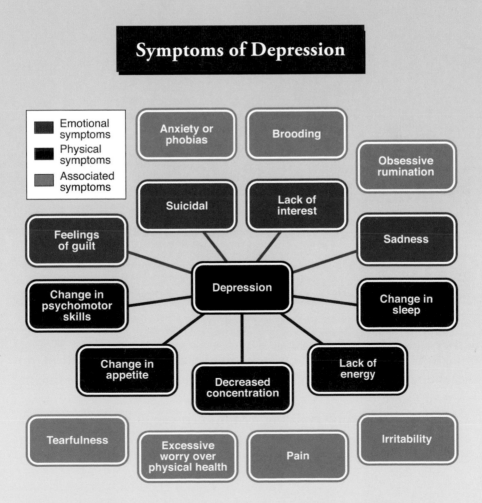

Taken from: Nicole Bullock. "Depressed Bloggers Anonymous." Beauty and the Bypass, March 8, 2010.

The author relates how unsuccessful dieting experiences led her into deep unhappiness.

it. Most of us can assign it enough power that I'm surprised the damn scale doesn't bellow, "TEN POINTS HUFFLEPUFF!" every time someone steps upon it.

Realizing this, fully realizing it, and then recognizing it to be true every day is harder than anything I have ever done and I am not always successful. But the flip side of that coin is that these days—at almost 30—I'm happier than I have been in a long time, because the things I used to assume were only fixable by banishing my boobs, my hips (which seldom, if ever, lie) and my butt, I've started tackling in other ways.

I've sort of had to accept that I am never going to be one of those people who is all, "This Baby Ruth [candy bar] is toooo rich." I'm always going to think about food I'm eating whenever I eat it, but it doesn't have to be in the combative self-destructive [way] I used to.

What I'm saying is, I'll finish that Baby Ruth for you—happily.

EVALUATING THE AUTHOR'S ARGUMENTS:

The author of this viewpoint, Rebecca Jane Stokes, suggests, from extensive details about her own experiences with dieting and weight loss, that dieting will not improve one's feelings about one's own weight and appearance, and can in fact lead to a cycle of unhappiness. Do you think the author is convincing in her argument? Why or why not?

Habitual Use of Social Media Sites Can Lead to Depression

Samantha Parent Walravens

"While Facebook offers a way to connect socially, in many ways it does the exact opposite. It prevents true intimacy."

In the following viewpoint Samantha Parent Walravens explains how her over-use of Facebook led to feelings of anxiety and depression. She writes about how she was the victim of someone's online rants and how that created feelings of helplessness in her. Walravens then goes on to discuss how teens sometimes feel the need to constantly update their Facebook profile to seem "cooler," causing depression and loss of self. She warns of some hidden dangers to watch out for when using social media sites such as Facebook and cautions teens and adults to use Facebook and other social media sites to connect with others but not to let those others control one's life. Samantha Parent Walravens is the author of *Torn: True Stories of Kids, Career & the Conflict of Modern Motherhood.*

AS YOU READ, CONSIDER THE FOLLOWING QUESTIONS:

1. In the article the author cites a book by MIT Professor Sherry Turkle who says that constant tweaking of a Facebook profile can lead to what kind of anxiety?
2. Walravens suggests that teens do what, instead of displaying all their emotions for the world to see?
3. What did a study by The Center for Eating Disorders find out can happen to young women that look at Facebook photos, according to the author?

I just deactivated my Facebook account, and I already feel my inner spirits rising anew—unencumbered by the "pokes" and "likes" of my 600+ social media "friends."

I created my Facebook page a year ago for professional purposes. As a business tool, it worked well. I used it to promote my new book, post upcoming readings and events and create an online community for readers to discuss the subject of my book—motherhood and the work-life juggle.

More Facebook Time Equals More Unhappiness

It wasn't until I let my Facebook page morph from professional to personal use that I encountered its nefarious side. I found that the more time I spent on Facebook, the unhappier I felt. It didn't help that I was also the victim of a disparaging rant on a woman's Facebook page—a woman I had never met. Since I wasn't Facebook "friends" with her, I couldn't respond to the post or do anything to stop it. It left me feeling beat up and helpless.

Let's face it: Facebook has forever changed the way that we interact with others. While it isn't all bad—it allows you to make new friends, stay in touch with old friends and connect with family members that you haven't seen in a while—it has an all-too-real dark side. Whereas a snarky comment made in passing can be erased from your memory, a posting on Facebook—be it a picture or a criticism—can go "viral" and become devastating for those targeted.

Nobody is immune. If you are on Facebook or other social media sites, you, too, are fair game.

In her book, *Alone Together: Why We Expect More from Technology and Less from Each Other,* MIT [Massachusetts Institute of Technology] Professor Sherry Turkle discusses the exhaustion felt by teenagers as they constantly change their Facebook profiles to appear "cool." For adolescents who are just forming their sense of self, this becomes a type of "performance anxiety" in which they feel that they are constantly on stage for others to view. The book's broader theory is that technology, despite its promises to bring us closer together, actually make us feel more isolated and alone. While Facebook offers a way to connect socially, in many ways it does the exact opposite. It prevents true intimacy.

I'm not advising everyone to deactivate their Facebook accounts. Just proceed with caution.

Some Things to Be Aware of When Using Facebook

Here are some of the hidden dangers of Facebook to watch out for:

1. Displaying your emotions for the world to see. With Facebook, it's too easy to disclose your struggles and opinions to the world, rather than confiding in a close-knit group of friends. Ranting about a person online is never a good idea. Posting defamatory statements on Facebook can result in a libel lawsuit. If you are angry or upset about something, documenting those private thoughts on Facebook can lead to embarrassment or trouble down the line. Better to talk to a close friend or therapist offline if you need to vent strong emotions.

2. Thinking Facebook "friends" are true friends. Let's face it: Most Facebook friendships are missing deep personal connections. You may feel that you are "connecting" with friends when you post or comment online. But spending time online takes away from the precious human interaction we get when we spend

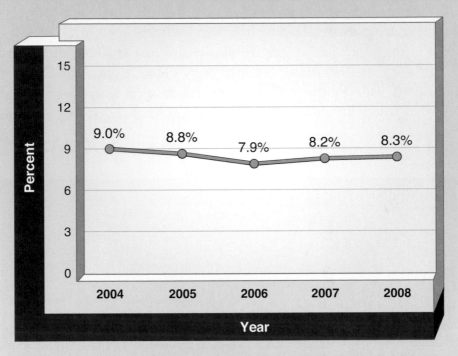

Prevalence of Depression Among US Youth, Ages Twelve to Seventeen (2004–2008)

9.0% 8.8% 7.9% 8.2% 8.3%

Percent

Year

Taken from: National Institute of Mental Health. "Major Depressive Disorder in Children." Data from the Substance Abuse and Mental Health Services Administration. *Results from the 2008 National Survey of Drug Use and Health.* http://samhsa.gov/data/nsduh/2k8nsduh/2k8Results.pdf.

time with our friends—in the flesh. Nothing beats the human touch.

3. Posting without thinking about who will read your post. I do college interviews for my alma mater, and I can tell you that I check applicants' Facebook pages before I write up my reports. Don't be naïve and use Facebook to post inappropriate pictures or comments—it won't help you get into college or get a job after college. I've heard of people losing jobs because of what they've posted online—much of which is not an accurate or appropriate portrayal of who they really are. Be careful of what you put out there to the world—it is a reflection of your character.

4. Facebook addiction. You get onto Facebook for five minutes and emerge two hours later, having looked up old boyfriends and college classmates, none the better for it. Facebook is a time

suck. A recent study has shown that it may even have addictive qualities. Like a drug, the more you use it, the unhappier it can make you. Part of the problem is that it takes you away from the more uplifting and productive aspects of your life—like completing assignments, reading books or interacting with real people.

5. Using Facebook to seek the approval of others. Why didn't she "like" my new profile picture? Why didn't I get invited to that party—all my friends were there? Facebook is a breeding ground for insecurity and self-doubt. I cringe when I get on Facebook

Many people have found that spending too much time on social media sites can lead to depression.

and feel the desperation of teenagers hoping to be "liked" by their friends. It's depressing to seek out the approval of others—trying to get them to "like" or "share" your posts, videos or pictures. For many teens, Facebook can contribute to feelings of low self-esteem.

6. Contributes to negative body image issues. A new study by The Center for Eating Disorders at Sheppard Pratt [hospital] found that looking at Facebook photos made people, especially young women and girls, more body-conscious. Half of the people surveyed said that looking at Facebook friends' photos made them wish they had the same body or weight the person pictured. According to Dr. Harry Brandt, director of The Center for Eating Disorders at Sheppard Pratt, which conducted the study, "Facebook is making it easier for people to spend more time and energy criticizing their own bodies and wishing they looked like someone else."

7. To compare is to despair. Along these same lines, Facebook posting can turn into an unhealthy competition of who's prettier, more popular or has the better life. This is especially true for women. According to a study from the University of Texas at Austin, while men are more likely to use Facebook to share items related to the news or current events, women tend to use it to engage in personal communication (posting photos, sharing content "related to friends and family"). This may make it especially hard for women to avoid comparisons that make them miserable.

8. Cyber-bullying and the threat of public criticism. Facebook gives any person with an account the ability to hide behind their alter-ego while they publicly criticize, gossip about and even cyber-bully innocent victims. Often, the victim is helpless to stop the abusive comments. Facebook is a public forum, and abuse can go viral.

9. Facebook stalking. Have you ever had a random stranger try to talk with you on Facebook? I have, and it's scary. You have to be careful who you associate with on Facebook. Many people hide behind their online profiles, so you have no idea who you're really talking with. People abuse the platform for their own corrupt benefits.

10. Trouble with the law. Many people are arrested each year—for libel, sexual harassment, dissemination of child pornography and more—because of what they have posted on Facebook. The police use Facebook to solve crimes. Remember that your Facebook posts can be monitored by the authorities, even if you think they are private.

Bottom line? You can use Facebook, but don't let it use you. Don't post anything that you wouldn't want published on the front page of the newspaper. And don't let "social networking" take over the way you interact with others. There is no substitute for getting out from behind your computer screen or smartphone and forging deep, personal and meaningful connections with real human beings.

EVALUATING THE AUTHOR'S ARGUMENTS:

After reading Samantha Parent Walravens's viewpoint about the connection between social media and depression and thinking about your own experiences, do you think that overuse of social media sites like Facebook can cause depression in teens? Do you think that some teens are just more likely to develop depression with or without the use of Facebook? Explain, using examples to support your answer.

Viewpoint 6

Habitual Use of Social Media Sites Does Not Lead to Depression

"'Facebook depression' [is] a term that the authors simply **made up** *to describe the phenomenon observed when depressed people use social media."*

John M. Grohol

In this article John M. Grohol, the founder and CEO of the website Psych Central and an expert on mental health, picks apart a clinical report done by the professional journal *Pediatrics* on the subject of "Facebook depression." Grohol argues that the clinical report was nothing more than shoddy research done to promote the authors' bias on the issue. He cites contradictory studies done by reputable sources that suggest that there is no relationship between social media and depression. One study cited offers evidence that in some teens social media can help with feelings of depression. Grohol insists that many of the citations used by the researchers are from third-party sources, and some do not even make mention of social media or depression. The problem with this, Grohol writes, is that many media outlets are running the story and suggesting that Facebook and other social media sites are actually triggering depression in teens.

AS YOU READ, CONSIDER THE FOLLOWING QUESTIONS:
1. What does Grohol say is wrong with the citations *Pediatrics* uses in its clinical study?
2. According to the author, researchers found a correlation between the two factors of Facebook use and depression in what kind of people only?
3. One study cited by Grohol revealed that social media sites could actually lead to what?

You know it's not good when one of the most prestigious pediatric journals, *Pediatrics*, can't differentiate between correlation and causation.

And yet this is exactly what the authors of a "clinical report" did in reporting on the impact of social media on children and teens. Especially in their discussion of "Facebook depression," a term that the authors simply *made up* to describe the phenomenon observed when depressed people use social media.

Shoddy research? You bet. That's why *Pediatrics* calls it a "clinical report"—because it's at the level of a bad blog post written by people with a clear agenda. In this case, the report was written by Gwenn Schurgin O'Keeffe, Kathleen Clarke-Pearson and the American Academy of Pediatrics Council on Communications and Media (2011).

What makes this a bad report? Let's just look at the issue of "Facebook depression," their made-up term for a phenomenon that doesn't exist.

The authors of the *Pediatrics* report use six citations to support their claim that social media sites like Facebook actually *cause* depression in children and teens. Four of the six citations are third-party news reports on research in this area. In other words, *the authors couldn't even bother with reading the actual research to see if the research actually said what the news outlet reported it said.*

I expect to see this sort of lack of quality and laziness on blogs. Hey, a lot of time we're busy and we just want to make a point—that I can understand.

When you go to the trouble not only of writing a report but also publishing it in a peer-reviewed journal, you'd think you'd go to the trouble of reading the research—not other people's reporting on research.

Here's what the researchers in *Pediatrics* had to say about "Facebook depression":

> Researchers have proposed a new phenomenon called "Facebook depression," defined as depression that develops when preteens and teens spend a great deal of time on social media sites, such as Facebook, and then begin to exhibit classic symptoms of depression.
>
> Acceptance by and contact with peers is an important element of adolescent life. The intensity of the online world is thought to be a factor that may trigger depression in some adolescents. As with offline depression, preadolescents and adolescents who suffer from Facebook depression are at risk for social isolation and sometimes turn to risky Internet sites and blogs for "help" that may promote substance abuse, unsafe sexual practices, or aggressive or self-destructive behaviors.

Time and time again researchers are finding much more nuanced relationships between social networking sites and depression. In the Selfhout et al. (2009) study they cite, for instance, the researchers only found the correlation between the two factors in people with *low quality* friendships. Teens with what the researchers characterized as high quality friendships showed no increase in depression with increased social networking time.

The Study Ignored Contradictory Research

The *Pediatrics* authors also do what a lot of researchers do when promoting a specific bias or point of view—they simply ignore research that disagrees with their bias. Worse, they cite the supposed depression–social networking link as though it were a forgone conclusion—that researchers are all in agreement that this actually exists, and exists in a causative manner.

© Peter Broelman/Political Cartoons.

There are a multitude of studies that disagree with their point of view, however. One longitudinal study (Kraut et al., 1998) found that, over a period of 8–12 months, both loneliness and depression increased with time spent online among adolescent and adult first-time Internet users. In a one-year follow-up study (Kraut et al., 2002), however, the observed negative effects of Internet use had disappeared. In other words, this may not be a robust relationship (if it even exists) and may simply be something related to greater familiarity with the Internet.

Other research has shown that college students'—who are often older teens—Internet use was directly and indirectly related to less depression (Morgan & Cotten, 2003; LaRose, Eastin, & Gregg, 2001).

Furthermore, studies have revealed that Internet use can lead to online relationship formation, and thereby to more social support

([Nie and Erbring, 2000], [Wellman et al., 2001] and [Wolak et al., 2003])—which may subsequently lead to less internalizing problems.

In another study cited by the *Pediatrics* authors, simply reading the news report should've raised a red flag for them. Because the news report on the study quoted the study's author who specifically noted her study could not determine causation:

According to Morrison, pornography, online gaming and social networking site users had a higher incidence of moderate to severe depression than other users. "Our research indicates that excessive Internet use is associated with depression, but what we don't know is which comes first—are depressed people drawn to the Internet or does the Internet cause depression? What is clear is that for a small subset of people, excessive use of the Internet could be a warning signal for depressive tendencies," she added.

The other citations in the *Pediatrics* report are equally problematic (and one citation has nothing to do with social networking and depres-

The author disputes the studies that say social media use causes depression, claiming that such studies are flawed.

sion [Davila, 2009]). None mention the phrase "Facebook depression" (as far as I could determine), and none could demonstrate a causative relationship between use of Facebook making a teenager or child feel more depressed. Zero.

The Study Did Not Show That Facebook Causes Depression

I'm certain depressed people use Facebook, Twitter and other social networking websites. I'm certain people who are already feeling down or depressed might go online to talk to their friends, and try and be cheered up. This in no way suggests that by using more and more of Facebook, a person is going to get more depressed. That's just a silly conclusion to draw from the data to date, and we've previously discussed how use of the Internet has not been shown to *cause* depression, only that there's an association between the two.

If this is the level of "research" done to come to these conclusions about "Facebook depression," the entire report is suspect and should be questioned. This is not an objective clinical report; this is a piece of propaganda spouting a particular agenda and bias.

The problem now is that news outlets everywhere are picking up on "Facebook depression" and suggesting not only that it exists, but that researchers have found the online world somehow "triggers" depression in teens. *Pediatrics* and the American Academy of Pediatrics should be ashamed of this shoddy clinical report, and retract the entire section about "Facebook depression."

EVALUATING THE AUTHOR'S ARGUMENTS:

After reading Samantha Parent Walravens's viewpoint, which argues that social media sites can cause depression, and John M. Grohol's viewpoint that they do not, whose argument do you find more convincing? Are the negative feelings associated with Facebook use severe enough to be considered depression, or do people who are depressed sometimes use Facebook? Explain, using quotes from the viewpoints to support your answers.

Chapter 3

What Treatments Should Be Used to Address Depression?

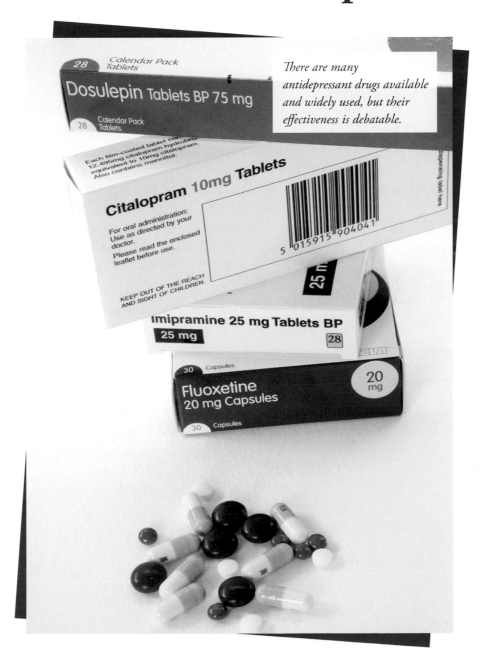

There are many antidepressant drugs available and widely used, but their effectiveness is debatable.

Antidepressants Help Relieve Symptoms of Depression

Thomas Sullivan

"Antidepressants help in severe depression, depressive subtypes, chronic minor depression, social unease and a range of conditions."

Thomas Sullivan argues in the following viewpoint that claims that antidepressant drugs are no more effective than a placebo are based on unreliable data and not grounded in science. He contends that studies aimed at delegitimizing antidepressants are not performed with the sort of diligence that is needed to determine whether antidepressants do in fact work. Further, he contends that sometimes these studies are funded by groups that do not have patients' best interests in mind. The danger of these kinds of studies, he maintains, is that they are influencing patients' and doctors' decisions on treatment options for depression. Sullivan is a former political consultant who in 1995 founded Rockpointe, Inc., a biomedical education company.

Thomas Sullivan, "In Defense of Antidepressants and All Other Seriously Researched Medical Products," *Policy and Medicine,* August 5, 2011. Copyright © 2011 by Thomas Sullivan. All rights reserved. Reproduced by permission.

AS YOU READ, CONSIDER THE FOLLOWING QUESTIONS:
1. According to a French study cited by the author, what were antidepressants particularly useful for treating?
2. What reason is given by Sullivan for the FDA's ability to identify useful medicines?
3. What is one way to help mute the placebo effect in drug trials, as stated by the author?

R ecently, a number of articles have suggested that antidepressants are no more effective than placebos. Just last month [in July 2011], in an essay in *The New York Review of Books*, Marcia Angell-Relman, former interim editor in chief of *The New England Journal of Medicine*, favorably entertained the premise that "psychoactive drugs are useless."

Earlier, a *USA Today* piece about a study done by the psychologist Robert DeRubeis had the headline, "Antidepressant lift may be all in your head," and shortly after, a *Newsweek* cover piece discussed research by the psychologist Irving Kirsch arguing that the drugs were no more effective than a placebo.

To address the controversy surrounding the effectiveness of antidepressants used in America, Peter D. Kramer, a clinical professor of psychiatry at Brown University, wrote an article in *The New York Times*, "defending antidepressants."

There Is Proof That Antidepressants Work

Kramer starts out by asserting that, "antidepressants work—ordinarily well, on a par with other medications doctors prescribe." He noted that, "certain researchers who have questioned their efficacy in particular areas," have done so "on the basis of shaky data."

The problem with these researchers using shaky data is that the notion that antidepressants "aren't effective in general is influencing treatment."

Kramer first offers support that antidepressants work from a study in France of more than 100 people with a particular kind of stroke. Along with physiotherapy, half received Prozac, and half a placebo. Members of the Prozac group recovered more of their mobility.

Antidepressants are good at treating post-stroke depression and good at preventing it. They also help protect memory. In stroke patients, antidepressants look like a tonic for brain health.

What was surprising to Kramer was that a friend of his, who suffered from a stroke, was not put on antidepressants until after Kramer himself emailed his friend's doctor. And even then, he learned from his friend, Robert G. Robinson at the University of Iowa's department of psychiatry, that neurologists say they "don't use an antidepressant unless a patient is suffering very serious depression" because "they're influenced by reports that say that's all antidepressants are good for."

Kramer asserts that, "the serious dispute about antidepressant efficacy has a limited focus. Do they work for the core symptoms (such as despair, low energy and feelings of worthlessness) of isolated episodes of mild or moderate depression? The claim that antidepressants do nothing for this common condition—that they are merely placebos with side effects—is based on studies that have probably received more ink than they deserve."

A woman consults with her doctor about her depression. Many doctors find antidepressants help their patients.

Critiques of Antidepressant Lack Evidence

Kramer points out that the most widely publicized debunking research—the basis for the *Newsweek* and *New York Review* pieces—is drawn from data submitted to the Food and Drug Administration (FDA) in the late 1980s and the 1990s by companies seeking approval for new drugs. This research led to its share of scandal when a study in *The New England Journal of Medicine* found that the trials had been published selectively. Papers showing that antidepressants work had found their way into print; unfavorable findings had not.

In his book *The Emperor's New Drugs: Exploding the Antidepressant Myth*, Dr. Kirsch, a psychologist at the University of Hull in England, analyzed all the data. He found that while the drugs outperformed the placebos for mild and moderate depression, the benefits were small. The problem with the Kirsch analysis—and none of the major press reports considered this shortcoming—is that the FDA material is ill suited to answer questions about mild depression.

Kramer explained that as a condition for drug approval, the FDA requires drug companies to demonstrate a medicine's efficacy in at least two trials. Trials in which neither the new drug nor an older, established drug is distinguishable from a placebo are deemed "failed" and are disregarded or weighed lightly in the evaluation. Consequently, companies rushing to get medications to market have had an incentive to run quick, sloppy trials.

Often subjects who don't really have depression are included—and (no surprise) weeks down the road they are not depressed. People may exaggerate their symptoms to get free care or incentive payments offered in trials. Other, perfectly honest subjects participate when they are at their worst and then spontaneously return to their usual, lower, level of depression. Kramer explained that these problems are an "artifact of the recruitment process." As a result, he noted that if many subjects labeled mildly depressed in the FDA data don't have depression, this would explain why they might respond to placebos as readily as to antidepressants.

Trials Present Evidence Supporting Antidepressants

Kramer explained how there are two sorts of studies that are done on drugs: broad trials and narrow trials. Broad trials, like those done to evaluate new drugs, can be difficult these days, because many antidepressants are available as generics.

Narrow studies, done on those with specific disorders, tend to be more reliable. Recruitment of subjects is straightforward; no one's walking off the street to enter a trial for stroke patients. Narrow studies have identified many specific indications for antidepressants, such as depression in neurological disorders, including multiple sclerosis and epilepsy; depression caused by interferon, a medication used to treat hepatitis and melanoma; and anxiety disorders in children.

New ones regularly emerge. The June [2011] issue of *Surgery Today* features a study in which elderly female cardiac patients who had had emergency operations and were given antidepressants experienced less depression, shorter hospital stays and fewer deaths in the hospital.

Broad studies tend to be most trustworthy when they look at patients with sustained illness. A reliable finding is that antidepressants work for chronic and recurrent mild depression, the condition called dysthymia. More than half of patients on medicine get better, compared to less than a third taking a placebo. (This level of efficacy—far from ideal—is typical across a range of conditions in which antidepressants outperform placebos.) Similarly, even the analyses that doubt the usefulness of antidepressants find that they help with severe depression.

In fact, antidepressants appear to have effects across the depressive spectrum. Scattered studies suggest that antidepressants bolster confidence or diminish emotional vulnerability—for people with depression but also for healthy people. In the depressed, the decrease in what is called neuroticism seems to protect against further episodes. Because neuroticism is not a core symptom of depression, most outcome trials don't measure

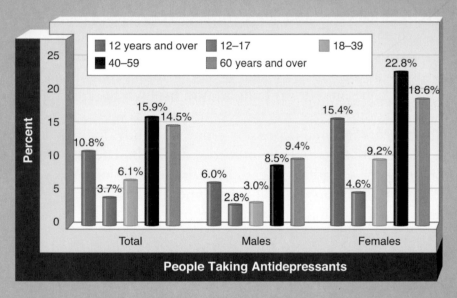

Percentage of People Twelve Years and Older Who Take Antidepressants, by Age, 2005–2008

Taken from: Laura A. Pratt, Debra J. Brody, and Qiuping Gu. "Antidepressant Use in Persons Aged 12 and Over: United States, 2005–2008." NCHS Data Brief, no. 76, October 2011. www.cdc.gov.

this change, but we can see why patients and doctors might consider it beneficial.

Similarly, in rodent and primate trials, antidepressants have broad effects on both healthy animals and animals with conditions that resemble mood disruptions in humans.

One reason the FDA manages to identify useful medicines is that it looks at a range of evidence. It encourages companies to submit "maintenance studies." In these trials, researchers take patients who are doing well on medication and switch some to dummy pills. If the drugs are acting as placebos, switching should do nothing. In an analysis that looked at maintenance studies for 4,410 patients with a range of severity levels, antidepressants cut the odds of relapse by 70 percent. These results, rarely referenced in the antidepressant-as-placebo literature, hardly suggest that the usefulness of the drugs is all in patients' heads.

The other round of media articles questioning antidepressants came in response to a seemingly minor study engineered to highlight placebo responses. One effort to mute the placebo effect in drug trials involves using a "washout period" during which all subjects get a dummy pill for up to two weeks. Those who report prompt relief are dropped; the study proceeds with those who remain symptomatic, with half getting the active medication. In light of subject recruitment problems, this approach has obvious appeal.

Consequently, Kramer explained how a study conducted by Dr. DeRubeis, an authority on cognitive behavioral psychotherapy, was problematic because it was built around his own research. Overall, the medications looked best for very severe depression and had only slight benefits for mild depression—but this study, looking at weak treatments and intentionally maximized placebo effects, could not quite meet the scientific standard for a firm conclusion. And yet, the publication of the no-washout paper produced a new round of news reports that antidepressants were placebos.

Drug Research Is Intensive and Extensive

In the end, Kramer asserted that, "the much heralded overview analyses look to be editorials with numbers attached. The intent, presumably to right the balance between psychotherapy and medication in the treatment of mild depression, may be admirable, but the data bearing on the question is messy."

As for the news media's uncritical embrace of debunking studies, Kramer suggested that this trend is based on a number of forces, including, "misdeeds—from hiding study results to paying off doctors—that have made Big Pharma an inviting and, frankly, an appropriate target."

That said, the result that the debunking analyses propose remains implausible: antidepressants help in severe depression, depressive subtypes, chronic minor depression, social unease and a range of conditions modeled in mice and monkeys—but uniquely not in isolated episodes of mild depression in humans.

Accordingly, Kramer noted that better-designed research may tell us whether there is a point on the continuum of mood disorder where antidepressants cease to work. Nevertheless, he recognized that "it is dangerous for the press to hammer away at the theme that antidepressants are placebos" because they are not, and to give the impression that they are is to cause needless suffering.

As far as other products [go], the effort that goes into researching a prescription product or medical device is amazing. Perhaps some of that effort should be considered when judging products.

EVALUATING THE AUTHOR'S ARGUMENTS:

Do you agree with the author Thomas Sullivan, that antidepressants have gotten a bad rap lately, or do you think that antidepressants are not as effective as drug companies would like the public to believe? Do you think the benefits of antidepressants are too great to overlook? Explain your answers.

Antidepressants Have Negative Health Consequences

Elizabeth Renter

> *"Anti-depressants have . . . been linked to increased risk of autism in children, higher rates of breast cancer, and even bone density depletion."*

As antidepressant drug use has increased, many individuals have expressed concern about the impact of these drugs on individuals' health in both the short and long term. Elizabeth Renter expands on this stance in the following viewpoint and expresses concern about the widespread use of antidepressants in the United States. Renter argues that the serious side effects and potential long-term health consequences make taking antidepressants more risky than beneficial. This risk is especially serious, she maintains, because the severity of the long-term health impacts is not fully understood since only minimal testing has been conducted thus far. Due to these risks and the belief that other interventions are more successful at treating depression, Renter endorses treatments such as proper diet and regular exercise as alternatives to drugs. Renter is a writer whose work focuses on natural health and criminal justice and has been featured in a number of online publications.

The number of people taking antidepressants has skyrocketed 400 percent from 2005 to 2008. They are the most widely used drugs in the United States, with a whopping 11 percent of Americans over the age of 12 taking them under a doctor's supervision. But, because antidepressants are relatively new medications and their massive prevalence is a recent phenomenon, little is known about both the short- and long-term effects of these drugs.

An estimated one-in-ten people report suffering from depression, and let's be clear—depression is not a situational sadness, it is a lasting and pervasive mood disorder.

However, many experts question its classification as a true disease, stating that there is no clear evidence that the "chemical imbalance" many doctors blame for the symptoms of depression actually exists at all. This aside, many people rely on prescription drugs to treat their depression, sometimes not fully understanding the risks involved with their medication.

> **FAST FACT**
>
> A 2011 report by the Centers for Disease Control and Prevention found that about one in twenty-five teens in the United States take antidepressants.

There are several different, widely used medications prescribed for the treatment of depression. The most common antidepressants are known as SSRIs, or selective serotonin reuptake inhibitors. They work by limiting the reuptake of serotonin in the brain. This reportedly assists in the management of depression because it's suspected that low levels of serotonin (the feel-good brain chemical) is associated with depressive symptoms. By preventing reuptake, more of the chemical is circulating in the brain. These drugs include Zoloft, Prozac, Celexa, Paxil and Lexapro.

Numerous Side Effects Accompany Antidepressants

As with all modern medications, there is a laundry list of potential side effects with antidepressants. These are the effects that are rattled off on commercials—the effects that lead you to wonder if the potential benefits justify the potential risks.

They include:

- Dry mouth
- Insomnia
- Nausea
- Drowsiness
- Diarrhea
- Dizziness

- Lack of sex drive
- Loss of appetite
- Weight gain
- Constipation
- Sweating
- Anxiety

These effects of antidepressants are often most noticeable when you first begin taking the prescription. As the body adjusts to the chemicals within the drug, the effects will reportedly become less noticeable.

Long-Term Effects of Antidepressants Are Unknown

The long-term effects of antidepressants are largely unknown. This is because most of these drugs haven't been in circulation for very long, and of those that have—few *unbiased* (not funded by the drug manufacturers) studies have been conducted. However, research has found the following to be possible long-term effects of antidepressants use:

Increased stroke risk: A study published in the journal *Neurology* indicated that patients taking SSRI drugs have a 50 percent greater chance of suffering an intracranial hemorrhage and a 40 percent greater risk of suffering an intracerebral hemorrhage when compared with people not taking antidepressants.

Thicker arteries: Potentially the cause of the increased stroke risk and additional risk of heart disease, scientists have found that taking SSRI drugs can increase the thickness of your arteries. Even when other standard heart disease risk factors were taken into consideration, scientists found that those who use antidepressants generally have thicker arteries, boosting the risk of related arterial diseases.

Birth defects and miscarriages: The FDA's [Food and Drug Administration's] MedWatch Adverse Events Reporting System reported that antidepressant use by pregnant women suffering from depression was responsible for more than 4,000 critical birth defects

Antidepressants are said to increase the risk of miscarriage by 68 percent.

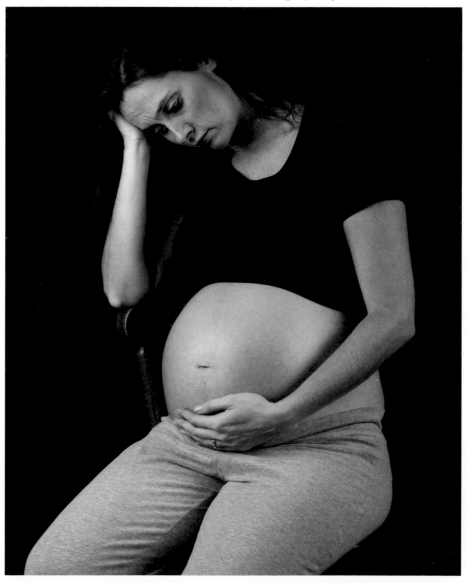

Types of Antidepressants and Common Side Effects

Antidepressant	Common Side Effects
Tricyclics	Tremors, indigestion, headache, dry mouth, drowsiness, elevated heart rate
SSRIs (selective serotonin reuptake inhibitors)	Sweating, indigestion, nausea headache, dry mouth, drowsiness, sexual side effects
SNRIs serotonin-norepinephrine reuptake inhibitors)	Tremors, nausea, headache, dry mouth, blurred vision, increased blood pressure, sexual side effects, nervousness, dizziness
MAOIs (monoamine oxidase inhibitors)	Insomnia, muscle aches, low blood pressure, dry mouth, sexual side effects, nervousness, dizziness, need to avoid decongestants and certain foods (fish, chocolate, fermented foods)
Newer Combinations	Appetite changes, indigestion, constipation, headache, dry mouth, insomnia, sweating, nervousness, sexual side effects, vomiting

Taken from: A. Page. "Taking Antidepressants: Myths vs. Facts." Health Central, May 2, 2012. www.healthcentral.com.

and heart defects, almost 3,000 spontaneous abortions, and 3,000 premature births. In all, antidepressants are said to increase the risk of miscarriage by 68 percent.

Suicide: Tragically ironic, many studies have linked the use of anti-depressants with an increased risk of suicide, suicide attempts and even worse depression symptoms.

Sudden cardiac death: Women who take antidepressants are twice as likely to suffer sudden cardiac death than those not on the medications.

Antidepressants have also been linked to increased risk of autism in children, higher rates of breast cancer, and even bone density depletion.

Antidepressants Do Not Provide the Most Effective Treatment for Depression

There are risks to taking any prescription drug. But people often accept those risks as par for the course—believing a doctor's advice is the best advice there is.

While antidepressants may provide much needed help to millions of people, they could also be harming us in yet-unknown ways. What we *do* know, however, is that some types of therapy has been proven even more effective than antidepressants, and that both a proper diet and regular exercise can go a long way in regulating mood and improving mental status without drugs.

EVALUATING THE AUTHOR'S ARGUMENTS:

After reading the viewpoints on the benefits of antidepressants by Thomas Sullivan in the previous viewpoint and the risks of antidepressants by Elizabeth Renter in this viewpoint, which view do you find more convincing? Do you think it is worth taking antidepressants in light of these risks, or is it better to explore alternative methods of treatment? Explain your view using examples from the viewpoints.

Antidepressants Cause Suicide and Violence

Peter Breggin

> *"[There are] dozens of dramatic cases in which peace-loving citizens have become suicidal, violent and psychotic from taking anti-depressant drugs."*

In recent years the number of suicides committed by members of the armed forces has risen dramatically. In the following viewpoint psychiatrist Peter Breggin places much of the blame on antidepressants for these suicides and the violence exhibited not only by military members but also the public at large. He outlines the increased use of antidepressants as opposed to therapeutic and educational programs to treat soldiers coping with trauma from battle and contends that instead of helping to solve the individuals' problems, these prescription drugs only create more. Chief among these problems are suicide and increased aggression, two side effects Breggin claims the drug companies work hard to cover. In opposition to this normal course of treatment, the author advocates for more therapeutic, family, and spiritual methods of overcoming depression, all focused on restoring hope. In addition to practicing psychiatry, Breggin serves as a consultant and medical expert in medical and product-liability lawsuits.

AS YOU READ, CONSIDER THE FOLLOWING QUESTIONS:
1. According to the army sources cited by the author, how has antidepressant drug use in the armed forces changed and to what effect?
2. What four facts does Breggin present to counter the claims presented by the "medical propaganda" on antidepressants?
3. What are the risks of stopping the use of antidepressants too quickly, according to Breggin?

Here are the starting [startling] facts: Death by suicide is at record levels in the armed services. Simultaneously the use of antidepressant drugs is also at record levels, including brand names like Prozac, Zoloft, Paxil, Celexa and Lexapro.

According to the army, in 2007 17% of combat troops in Afghanistan were taking prescription antidepressants or sleeping pills. Inside sources have given me an even bleaker picture: During Vietnam, a mere 1% [of] our troops were taking prescribed psychiatric drugs. By contrast, in the past year one-third of marines in combat zones were taking psychiatric drugs.

Are the pills helping? The army confirms that since 2002 the number of suicide attempts has increased six-fold. And more than 128 soldiers killed themselves last year [2008].

Antidepressants Do Not Help Soldiers

One theory states that the increased prescription of drugs is a response to increased depression among the soldiers. In reality, the use of psychiatric drugs escalates when, and only when, drug companies and their minions target new markets. In this case, the armed services have been pushing drugs as a cheap alternative to taking genuine care of the young men and women in our military. Instead of shortening tours of duty, instead of temporarily removing stressed-out soldiers from combat zones, and instead of providing counseling—the new army policy is to drug the troops.

There are many excellent therapeutic and educational programs for helping soldiers and veterans deal with war-related stresses. I recently addressed a national conference on stress in the military where I learned more about these approaches. I talked with many military officers and healthcare providers who want human services to replace the increasing prescription of psychiatric drugs. Some observed that the drugs often change the personality of the soldiers, making them irritable, edgy, and angry. They fear these drugs may unleash impulsive violence. Meanwhile, because many soldiers don't want to take psychiatric medications, they avoid seeking any kind of help.

Faith in Antidepressants Is Based on Myth

It's worth re-emphasizing that use of antidepressants is based more on myth than on science. Here are some proven facts totally at odds with medical propaganda:

First, there is no evidence that antidepressants prevent suicide and a great deal of evidence that they cause it.

Second, antidepressants almost never cure depression and instead they frequently worsen depression.

Third, antidepressants never cure biochemical imbalances. Instead, they always cause them. There are no known biochemical imbalances in the brains of depressed people until they start taking toxic psychiatric drugs and every person who takes one of these drugs ends up with a significant biochemical disturbance in the brain. That's how the drugs work—by disrupting normal biochemical processes in the brain.

Fourth, when all antidepressant studies are examined as a group, rather than cherry picked [carefully selected] by the drug companies, antidepressants are no better than placebo.

FDA [Food and Drug Administration] approval for an antidepressant requires that the drug companies produce only two positive clinical trials showing that the drug performs better than a sugar pill. So the drug companies carry out numerous studies using their more reliable paid hacks. Back at company headquarters, they then manipulate the data until they can make two studies look positive. Meanwhile, when all the studies are examined in what's called a meta-analysis, the

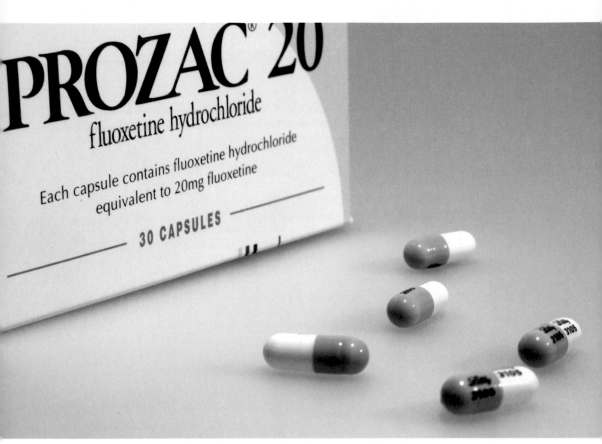

The author's research shows that patients have become suicidal, violent, and even psychotic from taking antidepressant drugs such as Prozac, Paxil, and Zoloft.

antidepressants are no better than a sugar pill. And of course, they are extraordinarily more dangerous.

Conclusion? Antidepressants are a hoax—in this case, a hoax that is killing members of our armed services.

Suicide and Aggression Are More than Side Effects

With billions of dollars at stake, the drug companies also do everything they can to downplay the risks of their products. Thus the pharmaceutical industry failed to find any evidence that antidepressants cause suicidality until the FDA forced them to re-evaluate their old data. The result? Now the FDA requires a black box warning [placed on the label or insert] that antidepressants increase the risk of suicidal behavior in children, youth and young adults. Limiting the risk to that age group is of course nonsense; these drugs cause suicidality in all ages.

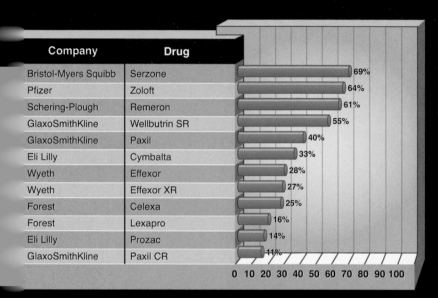

stimate of how much the impression of each drug's effectiveness
was inflated by not publishing unfavorable studies

Company	Drug	Estimated change in drug effectiveness (percent)
Bristol-Myers Squibb	Serzone	69%
Pfizer	Zoloft	64%
Schering-Plough	Remeron	61%
GlaxoSmithKline	Wellbutrin SR	55%
GlaxoSmithKline	Paxil	40%
Eli Lilly	Cymbalta	33%
Wyeth	Effexor	28%
Wyeth	Effexor XR	27%
Forest	Celexa	25%
Forest	Lexapro	16%
Eli Lilly	Prozac	14%
GlaxoSmithKline	Paxil CR	11%

0 10 20 30 40 50 60 70 80 90 100

**Estimated change in drug
effectiveness (percent)**

rom: *New England Journal of Medicine* from the article David Armstrong and Keith J. Winstein.
pressants Under Scrutiny Over Efficacy." *Wall Street Journal*, January 17, 2008.

ddition to suicide, the drugs cause a spectrum of adverse effects
e especially hazardous to soldiers who need the ability to control
motions, especially their frustration and anger. Many of the
common antidepressant side effects involve over-stimulation.
DA requires drug companies to list the following negative effects
ir descriptions of their antidepressant medications: "anxiety,
on, panic attacks, insomnia, irritability, hostility, aggressiveness,
sivity . . . and mania." We are giving our troops drugs that pro-
prescription for uncontrolled, disinhibited violence, including
on, irritability, impulsivity, hostility, and aggressiveness.

epression

In my latest book, *Medication Madness*, I describe dozens of dramatic cases in which peace-loving citizens have become suicidal, violent and psychotic from taking antidepressant drugs like Prozac, Paxil and Zoloft.

Meanwhile, as dangerous as it is to take antidepressant drugs, people should not rush into stopping them. After being exposed to these chemical agents for months or years, many people undergo agonizing emotional and physical withdrawal reactions. Some people crash into depression, some feel driven into anxiety, and others become irrationally angry. Many have bizarre neurological reactions like electric shocks in the head and weird feelings in their extremities. Withdrawal from antidepressants should be done gradually with experienced clinical supervision and the supportive involvement of family and friends.

Overcoming Depression Requires Hope

Despite all the emphasis of giving drugs to depressed people, many recover from depression with time on their own, while others receive help from a variety of sources, including therapy, family, and religion. Depression is a loss of hope. Depressed people are unable to see any ethical or viable options that will bring them happiness. They feel stymied, even emotionally paralyzed, because every choice seems bleak or overwhelming. They have given up. That's why, in the extreme, they sometimes want to die. They feel utterly helpless and hopeless in regard to making good lives for themselves.

The restoration of hope is key to overcoming depression and hope can come from many sources. The alternative to antidepressants is all of life: romantic love, family, friends, community, nature, and religion all help people overcome depression. Scientific studies show that everything from a new pet to an exercise program, as well as the passage of time, can relieve depression.

> **FAST FACT**
>
> In October 2004, after an extensive review of the effects of antidepressant medications on child and adolescent health, the Food and Drug Administration issued the requirement that all antidepressant packaging include a "black box" warning informing users of the heightened risk of suicidal thinking in youth taking these medications.

I explain to my patients: You have lost faith in your life—that you will ever love anyone or anything again. Getting over your depression will require pushing through your conflicts and fears, and finding the courage to love again—to love people, to love creative work, to love nature, and to love life.

Psychiatry Denies the Human Spirit

Modern biological psychiatry reflects and reinforces the worst in human values. Instead of liberating the spirit of overburdened and overwhelmed people, psychiatry denies and rejects the human spirit. It makes up fake biochemical theories that drive people [to] feel even more helpless. Most tragically, psychiatry then subdues the spirit by blunting the functions of the brain.

The principles for overcoming depression are exactly the same principles required for living a good and happy life. Good counseling offers an enthusiastic approach that inspires hope, while helping individuals to understand and to overcome their psychological barriers in order to exercise personal freedom, to take charge of their lives and to pursue happiness according to their own chose ethics and ideals.

I am not talking about unleashing a narcissistic approach—that kind of self-centeredness is more characteristic of depression itself. I'm talking about a whole-hearted embracing of life in which individuals overcome hopelessness, and renew their determination to take responsibility, to love, and to contribute to the family and community.

EVALUATING THE AUTHOR'S ARGUMENTS:

In his viewpoint Peter Breggin paints the drug companies who manufacture antidepressants as knowingly obscuring information about the possible dangers and side effects of the drugs. After reading his viewpoint, do you find any flaws in his argument? Does he go too far in his critique or not far enough? Explain.

Viewpoint 4

Holistic Approaches Are the Best Way to Treat Depression

James S. Gordon

"My treatment of choice is what many call 'Integrative.' I think of it as a way to get Unstuck, to help us move through and beyond the depression."

In the viewpoint that follows psychiatrist James S. Gordon details his seven steps to address depression. This multifaceted process tackles both physical and mental aspects of depression, and Gordon contends that only through this integrative approach can individuals with depression get "unstuck." He critiques the widely held belief that depression is a biochemical disorder requiring pharmaceutical intervention to balance out the body, and argues that the research does not support such an approach. In addition to practicing psychiatry, Gordon is founder and director of the Center for Mind-Body Medicine and the author of the book *Unstuck: Your Guide to the Seven-Stage Journey Out of Depression*.

AS YOU READ, CONSIDER THE FOLLOWING QUESTIONS:
1. What side effects do up to 70 percent of individuals taking SSRIs experience, according to the author?
2. What does Gordon define as the foundation of his "Unstuck approach"?
3. What are three of the methods given by the author that are essential to his integrative approach to depression?

A depression diagnosis does not have to be a life sentence. Often, it is a sign that our lives are out of balance and that we're stuck. It is a wake-up call and, potentially, the start of a journey that can help us become whole and happy, a journey that can change and transform our lives.

When a physician observes the signs and symptoms of "major depressive disorder" in someone—the difficulty sleeping and eating, the weight loss, the absence of interest in a world which once pleased her, the feelings of helplessness and hopelessness—he is likely to prescribe anti-depressant drugs. When a patient asks questions about the need for drugs, she (I use the feminine to remind us that more than twice as many women as men are diagnosed with depression) is often told, "Depression is a biochemical disorder like insulin-dependent diabetes. Diabetics need insulin because their pancreas doesn't work properly. And you need the drugs, the selective serotonin reuptake inhibitors (SSRIs), like Paxil and Prozac, to raise your levels of serotonin."

It sounds authoritative, appropriate, and effective. Unfortunately it's inaccurate.

Antidepressants Should Not Be the Treatment of Choice

First of all, the biochemical disorder has never been demonstrated. Some people with depression may have lower levels of serotonin, a neurotransmitter which helps to calm the brain and balance many body functions. But it seems that they are a minority. Doctors often don't even measure the level of serotonin before prescribing drugs to affect it.

Second, the SSRIs are not, in fact, selective. Serotonin producing cells are distributed widely through the brain and body—the small intestine has the largest number—and altering serotonin inevitably alters the level and action and many functions of other neurotransmitters, including dopamine, which mediates pleasure. A cascade of uncomfortable and sometimes dangerous side effects result, including gastro-intestinal upset, neurological problems like headaches, muscle stiffness and tremors, weight gain, and sexual dysfunctional—in up to 70 percent of all those who take the SSRIs. Indeed, in the early weeks of taking the drugs, a number of people, mostly young adults and adolescents, become more depressed and more suicidal.

In fact, neither the SSRIs, nor the serotonin-norepinephrine (norepinephrine is a neurotransmitter that may affect mood and activity level) reuptake inhibitors (SNRIs), which are increasingly prescribed, do a very good job. Doctors have prescribed these and other anti-depressants with great enthusiasm for more than twenty years—some thirty million Americans are currently using them for premenstrual syndrome, chronic pain, and anxiety, as well depression—because they believed the published studies which showed that the drugs were 60 to 70 percent more effective for depression than the placebos, the sugar pills, to which they were compared. These numbers were seriously misleading.

The author has found that practicing meditation is usually just as effective as taking antidepressants.

Top Ten Drug-Free Depression Treatments

1. Music therapy
2. Art therapy
3. Mindful meditation
4. Massage therapy
5. Group sports
6. Breathwork
7. Light therapy
8. Eye movement desensitization and reprocessing (EMDR)
9. Neurofeedback
10. Thai chi

Taken from: Alexandra Carmichael. "23 Surprisingly Effective Treatments for Depression (One Year Later)." *Cure Together Blog*, May 3, 2011. www.curetogether.com.

The drug companies, which profit hugely from SSRIs and other antidepressants, had, for the most part, only published the positive studies. When researchers went to the United States Food and Drug Administration and recovered the unpublished negative studies, the results were quite different. Reviews of the literature, which were published in our most prestigious medical journals—including *The New England Journal of Medicine* and *The Journal of the American Medical Association*—revealed that antidepressants were little, if any, better than placebos—except for a small minority of the most seriously depressed people.

All this doesn't mean that antidepressants aren't sometimes helpful. They can be, even with their limitations and side effects. What it does mean is that they should not be regarded as the "treatment of choice" as most physicians believe them to be, but instead as a last resort.

Integrative Treatment Is Best to Address Depression

My treatment of choice is what many call "integrative." I think of it as a way to get Unstuck, to help us move through and beyond the depression and the other difficulties that our lives may bring us. I describe this integrative, comprehensive approach in some detail in my book, *Unstuck: Your Guide to the Seven Stage Journey out of Depression*. It combines the best of conventional treatments, including various forms of psychotherapy, with a variety of other techniques that enhance each person's emotional life and cognitive abilities as well as her physical health. Medication should be used only when this approach doesn't work. "In extreme situations" [ancient Greek physician] Hippocrates said 2500 years ago "extreme remedies."

The foundation for this Unstuck approach is a meditative or mindful one—which simply means that it is designed to help people to be relaxed, aware and self-aware, and firmly grounded in the present moment. The Unstuck approach includes specific meditation techniques like slow, deep "soft belly" breathing and mindful walking and eating, which have been shown to decrease levels of anxiety and stress, enhance mood and optimism, and promote greater emotional stability and more reliable judgment. Both focused and mindful meditation raise the levels of the same neurotransmitters at which SSRIs and SNRIs are aimed.

Movement and exercise, which have been repeatedly shown to at least equal anti-depressants in relieving symptoms of depression, and also to raise neurotransmitter levels, are central. It looks like about 30 minutes of daily exercise is optimal, but all of us should start with what we can do—walking a couple of blocks is a great beginning—and be sure to do something we hope to enjoy.

Nutrition may also be crucial in preventing, as well as treating, depression. People who are depressed may be deficient in B vitamins, Vitamin D3, Selenium, Magnesium, and the Omega 3 fatty acids that are present in fish oil. Others are sensitive to gluten and other food substances which may cause inflammation, which has been implicated in depression.

It is important to stimulate imagination and intuition as well as nourish the body. I teach techniques like guided imagery, drawings, and written dialogues to help depressed and anxious people to access more easily their imagination and to use their intuition and creativity to find answers to previously insoluble problems.

Work with a skilled therapist can be important, even crucial, but it is exponentially enhanced by what we can do for ourselves. Because they are grounded in self-awareness and self-care, each and every one of these techniques carries with it a general as well as a specific benefit. In acting to understand and help ourselves, we overcome the feelings of helplessness and hopelessness that are the hallmarks of depression.

Many people find they can multiply the effectiveness of self-care by being part of a group in which they learn together and share their experiences and themselves with one another. In the Mind-Body Skills Groups which The Center for Mind-Body Medicine has developed, participants feel less like damaged or ill patients more like pilgrims together on a journey toward greater understanding, health, and wholeness.

Finally, symptom relief, the treatment of depression, and spiritual practice can be intimately connected. Using self-care techniques and living more meditatively often paves the way for us to connect with something—god, nature, a higher power—greater than ourselves and to find meaning and purpose in our lives. And spiritual connection, meaning, and purpose are among the most powerful proven antidotes to depression.

EVALUATING THE AUTHOR'S ARGUMENTS:

James S. Gordon's "Unstuck approach" utilizes many of the techniques used to combat depression that are described throughout this book, as well as adding some new ones. Do you think that this approach would work to help draw someone out of depression? Should an integrative approach be used instead of antidepressants? Explain your answers.

Music Can Help People Overcome Depression

Glenn Osrin

"With a LOT of Bon Jovi tunes, I was able to overcome massive depression and regain the ability to live and enjoy my life."

In the following viewpoint Glenn Osrin tells the tale of how Bon Jovi's music helped him regain the strength to take charge of his life and start to live again. Osrin explains how he lost his job and his health benefits and how this pushed him into a deep depression. One thing that he thinks also helped him was that he was very open to everyone about his struggle with his depression. He went to health professionals and received treatment for the illness, but nothing seemed to work until he began to listen to Bon Jovi. He believes that the music reprogrammed his brain and provided motivation for him to get back up and enjoy life again. Osrin is a music journalist.

AS YOU READ, CONSIDER THE FOLLOWING QUESTIONS:
1. What does Osrin believe led to his depression?
2. Besides listening to Bon Jovi, what else does the author attribute his recovery to?
3. What two things does the author say acted as a wake-up call for him?

Glenn Osrin, "How Bon Jovi Rocked My Depression into Submission," *Examiner*, August 20, 2010. Reproduced by permission.

Severe depression is like screaming under water.

Often coupled with relentless anxiety and sensitivity to light and sound, statistics show that many people never 'beat' depression. Data also shows—from the pharmaceutical companies themselves—that 7 out of 10 people prescribed medication for depression in the form of antidepressants or mood stabilizers do not get relief.

I should know, I was one of them.

That's why [as a Bon Jovi song goes] "this one goes out to the ones who mine for miracles; this one goes out to the ones in need". You see, once upon a time, horrific depression had me up against the ropes; literally holding on by my fingernails. But with good counseling, an adventurous medicine regimen until my doctor and I found the right combination that worked; and with a LOT of Bon Jovi tunes, I was able to overcome massive depression and regain the ability to live and enjoy my life.

Let's be perfectly clear: depression is a deadly-serious topic. This article does not profess to have all the answers; to be infallible or fool-proof, or, to make light of an affliction that can ruin lives and, in many cases, take them.

But for any fans out there of JoviNation in any part of the world who might be up against the same demons—or, are 'behind enemy lines' in your head like I was and can still be—it's important to hear what worked for someone else.

But before we get to the Bon Jovi factor, let me lay it out for you.

Serious Life Changes Can Lead to Depression

I spent 6 months lying in bed after losing a job I adored, wishing I would die. My wife would head out to work, and I would crawl back into bed and not wake up again until just before she came home. I literally walked around with a washcloth or a large, crumpled hand towel when I did go out because I was prone to breaking down and crying any time, any where.

Because I had lost my job and my medical benefits, I had to make the rounds of community health centers and other facilities that shall remain nameless simply just to get treatment. Let's just say these facilities made Jack Nicholson's *'One Flew Over the Cuckoo's Nest'* [movie set in a mental hospital] look like the Ritz Carlton.

Lifetime Prevalence of Depression in Thirteen- to Eighteen-Year-Olds

Lifetime Prevalence of Thirteen- to Eighteen-Year-Olds, by Severity

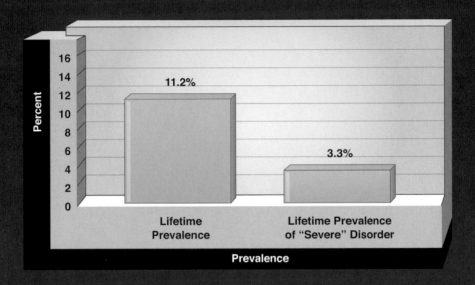

Demographics (for Lifetime Prevalence)

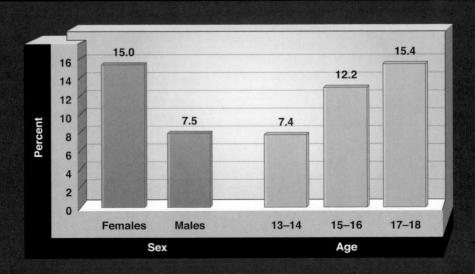

Taken from: National Institute of Mental Health. "Major Depressive Disorder in Children."

Speaking of cuckoo, I got so bad that I couldn't walk near my car in the garage at times because I constantly thought about putting myself to sleep with it; and, a belt for my pants hanging in my closet began to haunt me as well. So much 'noise' in my head, the ruminating on

Studies have shown that listening to music can relieve the symptoms of depression.

negative thoughts, the constant fear and loathing of myself and the circumstances I put my family in, all took their toll.

Fortunately for me, I wear my heart on my sleeve. Thus, I told anyone and everyone who would listen I was depressed; and, with the right professionals told them my deepest darkest thoughts about self-eradication.

That honesty and openness may have tested my wife and family—who tried bravely to fix and save me—but it saved me in every other way, because by talking about it, I was crying out for help, which meant in an odd way that I really didn't want to take myself out of life.

That said, through the wonders of modern pharmacology, a good doctor and an endlessly patient and loving wife, I was able to pull out of the deep, dark abyss of my mind. Two things acted as wake-up calls for me. The first was when a friend of mine who had recovered from depression told me so many times that I literally hated him that 'Depression can't hit a moving target'.

This meant getting my sorry ass out of bed every single day and doing something.

But the other notion that took hold is how very much my mind became like an old phonograph needle bumping and scratching against the same imperfection on an LP record; endlessly playing one part of the song over and over and over in my head until I was ready to jump out of my skin.

For me to get well, that thought process had to be literally re-grooved.

Music Can Motivate Individuals to Change Their Lives

This is where the music of Bon Jovi entered my life and helped me re-program, re-think, and re-charge my soul, saving my life in the process.

> ## FAST FACT
>
> The Cochrane Collaboration, a nonprofit organization that researches health care issues, reviewed five randomized trials of the impact of music therapy on depression and found that treatment plans that included music therapy were more effective at relieving the symptoms of depression than those that did not.

That's right, Bon Jovi—the Man and the Band—saved my life.

For the unfamiliar or the uninitiated to the wonders of all things Jovi, pick up virtually any Bon Jovi CD and you will hear songs of toughness in the face of obstacles, driving beats that kick up faith in the most unlikely places, and a tireless willingness to drink deeply of life; to embrace it; to conquer it; to turn it to our advantage; and most of all, to Live It.

All this from a little band of pretty boys who happened to survive the 80's glitter rock bonanza because of good hooks and incredible looks.

You see, I had started to make progress against the depression by kicking and scratching and teething and clawing my way back, and when I picked up the first couple of Bon Jovi CD's to listen to the songs I knew, I was astounded to hear the relentlessly positive message throughout the entire album catalog.

EVALUATING THE AUTHOR'S ARGUMENTS:

Rock journalist Glenn Osrin says that Bon Jovi saved his life. Do you believe that music can really be used to treat someone suffering from severe depression? How does this type of therapy compare with others described throughout this chapter?

Listening to Music Often Can Be a Marker for Depression in Teens

Beth Levine

"The more time teens spend listening to music, the more likely they are to be depressed."

In the viewpoint that follows Beth Levine reports the findings of a University of Pittsburgh study that found that teenagers who spend most of their spare time listening to music are more likely to be depressed. Levine cautions in her review that the study did not present, or even attempt to find, a *causal* link between teens' media use and depression, but the researchers did hypothesize that teens who chose to listen to music did so because they were depressed and sought an activity that required little exertion on their part. The author worries about these findings coupled with other research that has shown increased rates of depression compared with previous decades but remains optimistic that increased vigilance and knowledge can prevent teen depression from worsening. Levine is a health and wellness writer who has contributed to a variety of publications on diet, fitness, and well-being.

AS YOU READ, CONSIDER THE FOLLOWING QUESTIONS:
1. What were the most popular activities of teens diagnosed with clinical depression found in the study cited by the author?
2. According to Levine, how much time did the study find that teenagers listened to music, and how much more likely were these teens to be depressed?
3. As stated by the author, how does depression in teens today compare with depression in teens during the Great Depression?

Albert Einstein once said, "I get most joy in life out of music." And while that might seem like a beautiful sentiment, it doesn't necessarily jibe with the latest studies. According to new research, the more time teens spend listening to music, the more likely they are to be depressed.

Not All Media Use in Depressed Teens Is the Same

The study, which took place at the University of Pittsburgh, examined the relationship between depression in teenagers and the types of activities on which they spend the most spare time. The scientists gave 106 teenage volunteers cell phones, then used them to call the kids as often as 60 times during an eight-week period. The teens were asked to report what they were doing whenever a call was made. Close to half of the teenagers involved in the trial had received a diagnosis of clinical depression by a psychiatrist.

The reports on what the teenagers were spending their time doing was nothing surprising to either the researchers or parents of teens, since the vast majority of the teens spent a good chunk of their days absorbed in media. Television, computers, texting, and listening to MP3 players were the most popular activities. The most common way to while away the days was watching TV or movies, accounting for 26 percent of their time. Interestingly, there didn't seem to be much of a correlation between time spent watching TV and depression among teens, which contradicts the findings of previous studies.

The relationship between listening to music and depression, however, was very strong. Although the teenagers only spent an average of 9 percent of their time listening to music, those who spent the most time listening were found to be eight times more likely to be depressed than those who didn't listen as often. It should be noted that the study did not break down the types of music that teens listened

The author reports on a study that found that teens who excessively use media, especially to listen to music, are often depressed.

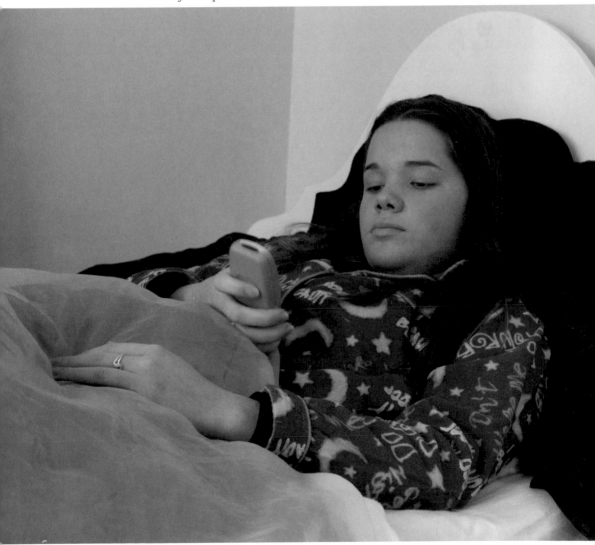

to and whether sonatas (as if many teens listen to sonatas) produced different results when compared to gangsta rap.

Listening to Music Increases Passivity

Now, that doesn't necessarily mean that the music is causing depression in these kids. In fact, the researchers made no attempt to identify cause and effect. The reason for the study was simply that depression is a major health problem for teenagers, so the researchers thought it was worth looking into. A better explanation of cause and effect in this case, according to the researchers, is that the teens are seeking comfort in the music and choosing an activity that really requires no effort on their part. (So it looks like Albert Einstein can rest in peace.) At the other end of the spectrum were the teenagers who spent the most time reading—which, sadly, only occurred a paltry 0.2 percent of the time. But the ones who were the most frequent readers were ten times less likely to be depressed as those who read the least. That could be because reading expends more mental energy than listening to music or watching TV—which might be indicative of a teen who is correspondingly more proactive, rather than passive, about the circumstances they confront in life.

This is not really good news, because we all know that teens spend a lot more time plugged into an iPod than they do with a good book or even a newspaper. And to make matters worse, a 2010 study at five universities found that teens and young adults are now far more depressed, unstable, and narcissistic than they were 70 years ago.

> **FAST FACT**
>
> The American Psychological Association journal *Psychology of Aesthetics, Creativity, and the Arts* published a study in 2013 that found that both male and female adolescents who participated in arts-related activities were more likely to exhibit depressive symptoms than those who did not participate in these activities.

Researchers analyzed psychological data compiled between 1938 and 2007 on students who took the Minnesota Multiphasic Personality Inventory (MMPI), a personality test that diagnoses mental illness and

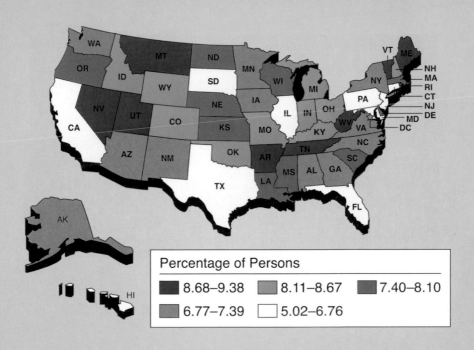

Major Depression Episodes Among Adolescents, by State

Percentage of Persons

■ 8.68–9.38	■ 8.11–8.67	■ 7.40–8.10
■ 6.77–7.39	□ 5.02–6.76	

Taken from: SAMHSA, Office of Applied Studies. National Survey on Drug Use and Health.

personality structure. According to the results, kids today are far more troubled than they were back in 1938, during the great Depression no less! Six times as many youths today test as clinically depressed compared to back then (six percent versus one percent), and six times as many register as anxious (five percent in 1938, but a whopping 31 percent now).

Since we're not likely to be prying our teenagers away from all things media-related any time soon, we may just have to be extra vigilant as parents. Maybe their music-listening habits can be a tool for helping us determine when they are getting depressed. And remember, it's not "necessarily" the listening to music that's the problem, but rather the amount of listening and the reason for the listening—passivity—that count. Given that, you might want to see if you can get your teens involved in some kind of regular physical activity. And in fact, there are studies that show that exercise works better than pharmaceutical drugs when it comes to relieving depression.

EVALUATING THE AUTHOR'S ARGUMENTS:

After reading this viewpoint by Beth Levine and reviewing the findings of the study presented, do you believe that listening to music is connected to depression? In your opinion, how do the findings of this study compare with the information presented by Glenn Osrin in the preceding viewpoint, who states that music saved his life? Explain your answer using quotes from the viewpoints.

Facts About Depression

Editor's note: These facts can be used in reports to add credibility when making important points or claims.

Prevalence of Depression

According to a survey conducted between 2006 and 2008 by the Centers for Disease Control and Prevention, it was found that roughly 9 percent of respondents in America met criteria for depression (3.4 percent for major depression). The age, gender, racial, and employment status of those reporting major depression break down as follows:

- 1.8 percent of individuals were 18–24 years of age
- 3.4 percent of individuals were 25–34 years of age
- 3.6 percent of individuals were 35–44 years of age
- 4.6 percent of individuals were 45–64 years of age
- 1.6 percent of individuals were over 64 years of age
- 2.7 percent were men
- 4.0 percent were women
- 3.1 percent were whites
- 4.0 percent were black
- 4.0 percent were Hispanic
- 2.0 percent were employed
- 9.8 percent were unemployed
- 1.6 percent were retired
- 22.2 were unable to work

In a 2007 report (based on evidence gathered between 2004 and 2005), the Substance Abuse and Mental Health Services Administration (SAMHSA) reported that, by state, the percentage of twelve- to seventeen-year-olds suffering from depression fluctuated from a low of 7.19 (in Louisiana) to a high of 10.37 (in Idaho). The statistical average was 8.88 percent for all fifty states.

Symptoms of Depression

According to the National Alliance on Mental Illness, common symptoms of depression include:

- changes in sleep, with some people experiencing difficulty falling asleep, waking up during the night, or awakening earlier than desired, whereas other people slept excessively or much longer than they used to;
- changes in appetite, with weight gain or weight loss demonstrating changes in eating habits and appetite during episodes of depression;
- poor concentration, the inability to concentrate and/or make decisions being a serious aspect of depression; during severe depression, some people find following the thread of a simple newspaper article to be extremely difficult or the making of major decisions to be often impossible;
- loss of energy, which along with fatigue often affects people living with depression; mental speed and activity are usually reduced, as is the ability to perform normal daily routines;
- loss of interest in usual activities;
- low self-esteem, dwelling on memories of losses or failures, and feeling excessive guilt and helplessness;
- hopelessness or guilt or a belief that nothing will ever improve; these feelings can lead to thoughts of suicide;
- movement changes in which depressed people may literally look "slowed down" or, just the opposite, overly activated and agitated.

The National Institute of Mental Health reports that suicide and attempted suicide are common risk factors in mental illness (including depression).

Treatment of Depression

Medications often prescribed to treat depression include:

- selective serotonin reuptake inhibitors (SSRIs) such as fluoxetine (Prozac), citalopram (Celexa), sertraline (Zoloft), paroxetine (Paxil), and escitalopram (Lexapro);

- serotonin and norepinephrine reuptake inhibitors (SNRIs) such as venlafaxine (Effexor) and duloxetine (Cymbalta); and
- unique nontricyclic antidepressant bupropion (Wellbutrin).

Antipsychotic medications often prescribed to treat bipolar disorders include: olanzapine (Zyprexa), aripiprazole (Abilify), risperidone (Risperdal), ziprasidone (Geodon), and clozapine (Clorazil).

Organizations to Contact

The editors have compiled the following list of organizations concerned with the issues debated in this book. The descriptions are derived from materials provided by the organizations. All have publications or information available for interested readers. The list was compiled on the date of publication of the present volume; the information provided here may change. Be aware that many organizations take several weeks or longer to respond to inquiries, so allow as much time as possible for the receipt of requested materials.

Adolescent Depression Awareness Program (ADAP)
The Johns Hopkins Hospital, Meyer Bldg., Rm. 3-181, 600 N. Wolfe St.
Baltimore, MD 21287-7381
(410) 502-3447 • fax (410) 955-0152
e-mail: adap@jhml.edu
website: www.hopkinsmedicine.org/psychiatry/specialty_areas
/moods/ADAP

ADAP is a program within the Mood and Disorders Center at Johns Hopkins University that works to educate high school students, teachers, and parents about depression using a student curriculum, training programs for health and school professionals, and parent and community presentations. The program seeks to deliver the message that depression and bipolar disorder are medical illnesses that can be treated if individuals seek help. Publications that ADAP makes available online include "Adolescent Depression: What We Know, What We Look For, and What We Do" and a curriculum outline.

American Academy of Child and Adolescent Psychiatry (AACAP)
3615 Wisconsin Ave. NW
Washington, DC 20016-3007
(202) 966-7300 • fax (202) 966-2891
website: www.aacap.org

AACAP seeks to provide treatment and make better the lives of the 7 million to 12 million American children and adolescents who experience mental, behavioral, and developmental disorders. Specifically, the organization publishes educational information on mental disorders and seeks to eliminate the stigma associated with these conditions. The organization provides a depression resource center on its website with sections including general information about depression, frequently asked questions, facts for families, and video clips.

Anxiety and Depression Association of America (ADAA)
8701 Georgia Ave., Ste. 412
Silver Spring, MD 20910
(240) 485-1001 • fax (240) 485-1035
website: www.adaa.org

ADAA is an organization focusing on education, training, and research on anxiety, obsessive-compulsive disorder, post-traumatic stress disorder, depression, and related conditions. The organization acts to raise awareness about these disorders and the impact they have on people's lives, pushing to advance scientific knowledge about what causes these conditions and how to treat them, and connecting people who need treatment with those who can help them. Its website provides extensive information about the symptoms, treatment, and current research being conducted on depression.

Centers for Disease Control and Prevention (CDC)
1600 Clifton Rd.
Atlanta, GA 30333
(800) 232-4636
website: www.cdc.gov

The CDC is the federal government agency charged with protecting American citizens' health and safety from threats arising naturally, from human mistakes, or as the result of calculated attacks. The organization covers all categories of health issues, including depression, and conducts surveys and research to provide information about the scope of the problem of depression. Statistics can be found on the CDC website along with research results regarding the best approaches to address depression.

Erika's Lighthouse

897 Green Bay Rd., #1–2A
Winnetka, IL 60093
(847) 386-6481
website: www.erikaslighthouse.org

Erika's Lighthouse is a grassroots organization that seeks to raise awareness about adolescent depression and mental health by producing educational materials and programs directed toward schools, teachers, parents, health care professionals, and teens. Many of these publications and programs focus on recognizing the signs of depression early and providing appropriate support to limit negative impacts on the lives of depressed teens and those around them. Information about programs such as the All School Teen Board, Teen Clubs, and Teen Panel Presentations can be accessed on the organization's website.

Freedom from Fear (FFF)

308 Seaview Ave.
Staten Island, NY 10305
(718) 351-1717
e-mail: help@freedomfromfear.org
website: www.freedomfromfear.org

FFF is a national nonprofit organization advocating since 1984 on behalf of individuals who suffer from anxiety and depression. The organization seeks to improve the lives of people living with anxiety, depression, and related illnesses. The FFF website provides an overview of anxiety disorders and depression, information about treatment options and how to find one that is right for each individual, and access to videos of the Mind in Motion mental health program.

Mental Health America (MHA)

2000 N. Beauregard St., 6th Fl.
Alexandria, VA 22311
(703) 684-7722; toll-free: (800) 969-6642 • fax (703) 684-5968
e-mail: info@mentalhealthamerica.net
website: www.nmha.org

MHA is a national nonprofit organization committed to assisting all Americans in their pursuit to live mentally healthy lives through its advocacy, education, research, and service programs. More than two hundred affiliates around the country work in cooperation to educate the public and promote policy reform and the adoption of effective prevention and recovery programs. The organization provides a wide range of information about depression both generally and in specific populations, including African Americans, older adults, teens, and women.

National Alliance on Mental Illness (NAMI)
3803 N. Fairfax Dr., Ste. 100
Arlington, VA 22203
(703) 524-7600 • fax (703) 524-9094
website: www.nami.org

NAMI has worked since its founding in 1979 to improve the lives of individuals around the nation living with mental illness through its advocacy efforts to increase access to services, treatment, support, and research. Depression is one of the many mental illnesses addressed by the organization, and general information about the condition as well as more detailed information focused on teens' experiences with depression can be found on the NAMI website. The *Advocate* is the official magazine of NAMI and is published three times a year.

National Institute of Mental Health (NIMH)
Science Writing, Press, and Dissemination Branch
6001 Executive Blvd., Rm. 6200, MSC 9663
Bethesda, MD 20892-9663
(301) 443-4513; toll-free: (866) 615-6464 • fax (301) 443-4279
e-mail: nimhinfo@nih.gov
website: www.nimh.nih.gov

NIMH is the national agency, operating within the National Institutes of Health, charged with advancing the understanding and treatment of mental illness by conducting clinical research. Depression is one among the many wide-ranging conditions researched by NIMH, and the institute's page on this condition includes a definition, causes, signs and symptoms, diagnosis, treatments, at-risk populations, living with depression, and clinical trials. Publications available online include the booklets *Depression* and *Depression and College Students* and the "Depression and High School Students" fact sheet.

World Health Organization (WHO)
Avenue Appia 20, 1211
Geneva 27, Switzerland
+41 22 791 21 11 • fax: +41 22 791 31 11
website: www.who.int

WHO is the United Nations agency in charge of all health-related initiatives within this international organization. Tasks of WHO include acting as a leader on health matters affecting people worldwide, providing research direction, establishing norms and standards, suggesting policy options based on sound research and evidence, and offering health assistance to countries in need. Depression is one of the many health topics covered by the organization. Resources on this condition available on the WHO website include a fact sheet, information about World Mental Health Day, "Depression—A Hidden Burden," and the video *I Had a Black Dog: His Name Was Depression*.

For Further Reading

Books

Beck, Aaron T., and Brad A. Alford. *Depression: Causes and Treatment.* 2nd ed. Philadelphia: University of Pennsylvania Press, 2009. Presenting depression as a cognitive disorder, this textbook looks at various causes, research models, and treatments of depression.

Jamison, Kay Redfield. *An Unquiet Mind: A Memoir of Moods and Madness.* New York: Vintage, 1997. A therapist explains how years of treating depressed and unstable patients paralleled her own bout with bipolar illness.

Kirsch, Irving. *The Emperor's New Drugs: Exploding the Antidepressant Myth.* New York, Basic, 2011. A research psychologist contends that the prescription of antidepressants is based on faulty science and the financial power of pharmaceutical companies.

O'Connor, Richard. *Undoing Depression: What Therapy Doesn't Teach You and Medication Can't Give You.* New York: Little, Brown, 2010. A psychotherapist argues that the habits that engender and support depression can be unlearned and overcome through a holistic approach to recovery.

Parks, Peggy. *Teen Depression.* Detroit: Lucent, 2013. This overview of the problem of depression in teenagers looks at the roots of the illness, its manifestations, and its treatments.

Real, Terrence. *I Don't Want to Talk About It: Overcoming the Secret Legacy of Male Depression.* New York: Scribner, 1998. Based on his own experience as a family psychotherapist and as a victim of a depressed father, the author examines male depression and the dangers of its transmission from one generation to the next.

Sharpe, Katherine. *Coming of Age on Zoloft: How Antidepressants Cheered Us Up, Let Us Down, and Changed Who We Are.* New York: Harper Perennial, 2012. While acknowledging the positives and negatives associated with antidepressant drug treatments, the author focuses on the role of antidepressants in a society seemingly addicted to prescription drugs.

Solomon, Andrew. *The Noonday Demon: An Atlas of Depression.* New York: Scribner, 2002. A victim of depression traces the science, treatment, and cultural politics of the disease, focusing on controversial therapies and the inconclusive biological and psychological models used to explain it.

Williams, Mark, et al. *The Mindful Way Through Depression: Freeing Yourself from Chronic Unhappiness.* New York: Guilford, 2007. Four doctors offer meditation and cognitive therapy as a means to avoid the mental stresses that lead to depression.

Periodicals

Baldauf, Sarah. "If the Gloom Won't Lift," *U.S. News & World Report,* December 2009.

Bartz, Andrea. "Prescription for Happiness," *Shape,* March 2012.

Begley, Sharon, and Sarah Kliff. "The Depressing News About Antidepressants," *Newsweek,* February 8, 2010.

Greener, Mark. "Beyond Serotonin: New Approaches to the Management of Depression," *Progress in Neurology & Psychiatry,* July 2013.

Grimm, Simone, and Milan Scheidegger. "A Trip Out of Depression," *Scientific American Mind,* May/June 2013.

Knaresboro, Tarah. "Pass It Along: Genes Alone Do Not Explain Depression in Families," *Psychology Today,* March/April 2012.

Levine, Bruce E. "Surviving America's Depression Epidemic," *Share Guide,* May/June 2011.

Maclean's. "The Broken Generation," September 10, 2012.

Miller, Michael Craig. "Exercise Is a State of Mind," *Newsweek,* March 26, 2007.

Mitchell, Kathleen. "Beyond the Baby Blues," *BusinessWest,* June 4, 2012.

Murphy, Samantha. "Rebuilding Broken Brains," *New Scientist,* July 27, 2013.

Puterbaugh. Dolores T. "Sad Teenage Girls Are Becoming More So," *USA Today Magazine,* March 2013.

Rosen, Margery D. "Sad Dads," *Parents,* April 2013.

Sanburn, Josh. "Comfort Creatures," *Time,* April 22, 2013.

Williams, Alexandra. "Link Between Poor Diet and Depression in Women," *IDEA Fitness Journal*, April 2013.

Websites

American Psychological Association (www.apa.org). The American Psychological Association is a professional association drawing together clinicians and researchers in the field of psychology. The organization's website contains a section on depression and related disorders. There, visitors can find links to information on the illness and links to scientific reports and articles that inform the growing body of knowledge on these illnesses. The website also provides information on how to get help for those who might be suffering from depression.

Anxiety and Depression Association of America (www.adaa.org). The association's website presents personal stories of people living with these illnesses as well as information on how to manage mood disorders. There are other links to assist visitors in finding therapists who can help diagnose and treat these problems.

Depression and Bipolar Support Alliance (www.dbsalliance.org). The alliance's website contains a workbook to aid individuals in determining progress in fighting these disorders and links to help find outside assistance.

Freedom from Fear (www.freedomfromfear.org). The Freedom from Fear website contains general information on depression and treatment options. It provides links to those seeking help and publishes a newsletter for subscribers.

More than Sad (www.morethansad.org). This website contains a fact sheet on the illness and a resource list for those seeking help as well as an available DVD on depression.

National Alliance on Mental Illness (www.nami.org). Theis website offers discussion forums on issues concerning teens and a wide array of links to publications and other outlets for educating visitors about depression and other mental illnesses.

National Institute of Mental Health (www.nimh.nih.gov). The National Institute of Mental Health (NIMH) website provides general information on depression, including its supposed causes and its treatments. Links connect visitors to current research and studies within the NIMH and in other scientific literature.

Index

Mercieca, Tamra, 32–33
Minnesota Multiphasic
    Personality Inventory
    (MMPI), 122–123
Monoamine oxidase inhibitors
    (MAOIs), side effects of, *98*
Music
    can help overcome
        depression, 113–118
    excessive listening to, can be
        a marker for depression in
        teens, 119–124

N
National Comorbidity
    Survey—Adolescent
    Supplement, 14
National Institute of Mental
    Health (NIMH), 8–9, 37
National Survey on Drug Use
    and Health (Substance Abuse
    and Mental Health Services
    Administration), 20, 27
Neurology (journal), 96
Neuroticism, 90–91
Neurotransmitters, 9
    coronary artery disease and,
        27
    folate and, 63
*New England Journal of
    Medicine,* 89, 110
The New York Review of Books
    (periodical), 87
New York Times (newspaper),
    87
Newsweek (newspaper), 87
NHS Choices (website), 47, 68

NIMH (National Institute of
    Mental Health), 8–9, 37
Norepinephrine, 25, 109
Nutrition, may be useful
    in preventing/treating
    depression, 64–65, 111

O
O'Connell, Bridget, 32, 34,
    35
O'Keeffe, Gwenn Schurgin,
    80
Omega-3 fatty acids, 62, 65,
    111
*One Flew Over the Cuckoo's
    Nest* (film), 114
Osrin, Glenn, 113
Osteoporosis, 27

P
Packard, Robert, 12
Page, Kailie, 39
Pain, can be manifestation of
    depression, 24–25
Pediatrics (journal), 80, 81
Placebos/placebo responses,
    91–92, 110
Plaisted, Haley, 37, 39–43
Postpartum depression, 9
Prozac (fluoxetine), 87–88,
    103
*Psychology of Aesthetics,
    Creativity, and the Arts*
    (journal), 122
Psychology Today (magazine),
    10
Psychotic depression, 9

WHO (World Health Organization), 7

Withdrawal, from antidepressants, 105

World Health Organization (WHO), 7

Y

Youth
antidepressant use and risk of suicide among, 105
depression is main cause of suicide among, 36–45
excessive listening to music can be a marker for depression in, 119–124
prevalence of depression among, 8, 14, 20, *75, 115, 123*
views on seriousness of suicide as health issue, *43*

Picture Credits

© AP Images/Josh Reynolds, 34

© BSIP SA/Alamy, 40, 57

© Catchlight Visual Services/Alamy, 70

© Nic Cleave/Alamy, 97

© Iain Cooper/Alamy, 103

© Culture RM/Alamy, 46, 109

© FocusDigital/Alamy, 83

© Gale, Cengage, 15, 21, 25, 43, 53, 64, 69, 75, 91, 98, 104, 110, 115, 123

© Sigrid Gombert/Science Source, 49

© David Hoffman Photo Library/Alamy, 88

© incamerastock/Alamy, 13

© Karel Lorier/Alamy, 121

© MB Images/Alamy, 76

© Hank Morgan/Science Source, 26

© Photo Researchers, Inc., 11

© Kumar Sriskandan/Alamy, 85

© SuperStock/Alamy, 19, 116

© Kristoffer Tripplarr/Alamy, 63